COLLEGE MINDFULNESS TRAINING

College Mindfulness Training is a ground-breaking book that carefully combines selected meditation exercises with guidance explaining the background, scientific context, and practical applications of mindfulness practice. More than just a meditation manual, this book details how and why personal mindfulness practice is essential for the college-aged student. In addition to extensive practical exercises for both beginner and intermediate-level meditation students, the author explores the kinds of institutions and organizations that have arisen out of the popular mindfulness movement and what career options in the field may be available in the future.

Throughout the manual, the author provides readers with insights into basic meditation techniques; active and passive meditation techniques; Focused Attention Meditation in both guided and self-guided forms; Open Monitoring Meditation; informal meditation exercises; a brief history of the MBSR program and Koru meditation; a survey of current apps and meditation-supportive technology platforms; and detailed instructions for self-driven practice, and a semester-long outline for teachers.

A captivating read, this book covers many of the essentials of mindfulness meditation and self-care of interest to college students, making it an essential tool for those of college age seeking to practice mindfulness meditation as well as college educators seeking a guided system to enhance their students' emotional well-being and academic performance.

Kevin Page is an author, theorist, and mindfulness pundit. He holds a Master's degree in psychology and has written two books on meditation practice for performing artists.

COLLEGE MINDFULNESS TRAINING

Reducing Student Life Stress and Improving Academic Performance

Kevin Page

NEW YORK AND LONDON

First published 2019
by Routledge
52 Vanderbilt Avenue, New York, NY 10017

and by Routledge
2 Park Square, Milton Park, Abingdon, Oxon OX14 4RN

Routledge is an imprint of the Taylor & Francis Group, an informa business

© 2019 Kevin Page

The right of Kevin Page to be identified as author of this work has been asserted by him in accordance with sections 77 and 78 of the Copyright, Designs and Patents Act 1988.

All rights reserved. No part of this book may be reprinted or reproduced or utilised in any form or by any electronic, mechanical, or other means, now known or hereafter invented, including photocopying and recording, or in any information storage or retrieval system, without permission in writing from the publishers.

Trademark notice: Product or corporate names may be trademarks or registered trademarks, and are used only for identification and explanation without intent to infringe.

Library of Congress Cataloging-in-Publication Data
A catalog record for this title has been requested

ISBN: 978-1-138-58424-2 (hbk)
ISBN: 978-1-138-58425-9 (pbk)
ISBN: 978-0-429-50613-0 (ebk)

Typeset in Bembo
by Taylor & Francis Books

For my mother, Joyce Page, who spent her life helping others.

You inspire me, Mama.

CONTENTS

Acknowledgments viii
Introduction: The Roots of CMT x

1 What Exactly Is Mindfulness? 1
2 Attention and Distraction in the Digital Age 22
3 What Is MBSR (and What It Is Not)? 32
4 Mindfulness in Everyday Life 48
5 Mind/Body Fitness 63
6 Apps, Gadgets, and Mindful Technology Use 73
7 Mindfulness Programs and Initiatives 80
8 Individual CMT Practice 94
9 CMT in an Institutional Setting 106

Appendix A: Sample CMT Course Syllabus 120
Appendix B: Research Articles and Book Resources 131
Appendix C: Organizations, Programs, and Apps 136
Index 143

ACKNOWLEDGMENTS

As with any book that endeavors to break fresh ground, *College Mindfulness Training* was made stronger and more complete by the contributions of several individuals and institutions. I cannot thank them enough, but I can acknowledge their assistance and generosity in making this effort possible.

First, to the many practitioners and compassionate teachers that generously took time from their personal and professional schedules to interview with me and provide basic research and insights into the teaching and propagation of mindfulness training particularly to a college audience in a university setting. These include, in no particular order: Steven Hickman (UC San Diego Center for Mindfulness), Holly Rogers (Center for Koru Mindfulness, Duke University), Yael Shy (Director of MindfulNYU), Aurora Casta (Counseling and Psychological Services at the University of Pennsylvania), Megan Leuchars Prager (UC San Diego Center for Mindfulness), Swati Desai (UC San Diego Center for Mindfulness), Bonnie Eckard (Arizona State University), Karen S. Newton (University of Louisville), Alexandra Morrison (California State University, Sacramento), and Roxanne Wright Stoehr (Southeastern Louisiana University).

I would like to thank my own meditation and mindfulness teachers and those that helped set me on this path of discovery (some of which I have only met through books). Again, in no particular order: Ruben Habito (founder of the Maria Kannon Zen Center), Susan Woods (Mindfulness-Based Professional Training Institute, UC San Diego), Kay Colbert (Dallas Yoga Center), Charles T. Tart (Institute of Transpersonal Psychology), Hillevi Ruumet (Institute of Transpersonal Psychology), and Ken Wilber (Integral Institute, author of *Integral Meditation*).

My editor at Routledge, Nina Guttapalle, and our wonderful editorial assistant, Olivia Powers. And my original acquisitions editor at Routledge, Lillian Rand.

Also, my theatre and performance studies editor at Routledge (who made the appropriate introductions to those that got this book off the ground), Stacey Walker.

A special thanks to the many authors, theorists, and publishers who have allowed me to quote from their copyrighted work in building my own case. (Parenthetical dates represent year of copyright notice.)

Page, K. (2018). *Advanced consciousness training for actors: Meditation techniques for the performing artist*. New York: Routledge. Reprinted with permission of Taylor & Francis; permission conveyed through Copyright Clearance Center, Inc.

Gorman, T.E. & Green, C.S. (2016). Short-term mindfulness intervention reduces the negative attentional effects associated with heavy media multitasking. *Scientific Reports*, 6, 24542. doi:10.1038/srep2454. www.nature.com/articles/srep24542#supplementary-information. This material is reprinted under the Creative Commons Attribution 4.0 International Public License.

Gazzaley, Adam & Rosen, Larry D. (2016). *The distracted mind: Ancient brains in a high-tech world*, pp. 8–9. © 2016 Adam Gazzaley and Larry Rosen. Reprinted with permission from the MIT Press.

Lepp, A., Barkley, J.E., & Karpinski, A.C. (2014). The relationship between cell phone use, academic performance, anxiety, and satisfaction with life in college students. *Computers in Human Behavior*, 31, 343–350. Reprinted with permission from Elsevier.

Ralph, B.C.W., Thomson, D.R., Cheyne, J.A., & Smilek, D. (2014). Media multitasking and failures of attention in everyday life. *Psychological Research*, 78(5), 661–669. Reprinted with permission from Springer Nature.

Kabat-Zinn, J. (2011). Some reflections on the origins of MBSR, skillful means, and the trouble with maps. *Contemporary Buddhism*, 12(1), 281–306. doi:10.1080/14639947.2011.564844. Reprinted by permission of the publisher (Taylor & Francis Ltd, www.tandfonline.com).

And finally, my family, Linda, Izzy, Jolie, Joyce, Monte, Michael, and Janet, and the personal friends that have supported me (in some cases for decades), you know who you are.

INTRODUCTION

The Roots of CMT

Creativity and the Silent Retreat

The impetus for this book was born out of a partially silent Mindfulness-Based Stress Reduction (MBSR) teacher training retreat held in Northern California in the spring of 2017. I was a participant in the retreat, part of an effort on my part to gain more understanding of how secularized meditation practice was imparted to various groups of people. By that time in my own research and training, I had been an on-again-off-again meditator for more than a dozen years, had studied a number of different types of meditation training during my graduate studies in psychology (which culminated in a Master's degree), and was just finishing up the manuscript of my first book on meditation training for actors. So, my background in this area was very diverse. The MBSR teacher training was intended to ground the participants in the basic protocol of the established (and very popular) eight-week Mindfulness-Based Stress Reduction class first developed by Jon Kabat-Zinn in the late 1970s (see Chapter 3). All of the retreat participants had already taken the eight-week course in MBSR in their home towns and now were interested in deepening their experiences and potentially becoming certified teachers of the technique themselves. As for myself, I was rather the odd-man-out, being a professional author and having little intent of teaching MBSR classes so much as understanding how and why this form of meditation study had become so popular and if there were a way to add those insights to my own writings.

My background as a meditation pundit is fairly unorthodox. During my own college days, I had studied theater and stage acting. Interestingly, much of the work done to train young actors for their work on the stage has to do with cultivating self-awareness and an awareness of sensations in the body, which is not dissimilar to meditation training in certain ways. This early awareness training would become important to me many years later when I began to study psychology. After a two-decade-long career as a film and television actor (IMDB, 2018) I entered graduate school to study the psychology of healthy functioning and development, growth potential, and consciousness. What I began to recognize in my explorations was a certain similarity to meditation training and the training of actors that led me to research and write two books applying meditation training in very specific ways that were intended to support actors and other performing artists in developing their creative talents (Page, 2018a, 2018b).

And so, by the spring of 2017, I found myself in an MBSR teacher training retreat, furthering my research while at the same time working on my own meditation practice. This retreat was somewhat unique. During the days, the participants attended classes that focused on the specific pedagogical structure of the MBSR program. Usually in the mornings we would experience the class activities (doing experiential exercises and participating in small-group discussions) and then in the afternoons discuss the details and best practices of how to teach this material to the average MBSR program attendees. MBSR, as discussed in Chapter 3, is a form of secularized meditation training (meaning it has been stripped of most of its original cultural or religious context, leaving the bare-bones experiential exercises more accessible to a Western audience) targeted mostly at medical patients with high levels of stress. Typical MBSR program candidates may be referred by their doctors or psychiatrists, often suffering from serious medical conditions such as cancer, hypertension, heart disease, depression, PTSD, etc., that can cause heightened levels of stress. Or, perhaps they are suffering directly from stress disorders and conditions of anxiety. In any case, the people that most often find themselves in an MBSR class are adults that are having problems, sometimes very serious problems, with stress, and the MBSR protocol is specifically designed to address that issue in an *adult population*. In the evenings and during all communal meals, the retreat shifted into a traditional silent mode of individual concentration and contemplation, the non-class hours filled with individual practice of the exercises we were studying during the day. As with most silent meditation retreats, the silence and inward turning of the attention in a disciplined and sustained fashion elevated the intensity of the experience. It was near the end of the six days of mostly silent contemplation, at sunrise on the fifth day while walking silently in a stone and gravel labyrinth focusing on my breathing, that the idea for a very specialized type of MBSR training sequence dedicated to college-aged students came to me in a creative flash.

Having just completed material that culminated the traditional MBSR protocol, I was struck by an important series of issues. First, meditation training, often now called "mindfulness" as a catch-all term, is proliferating in schools and colleges at expanding rates, part of a general "mindfulness movement" in our culture. Yet ways of teaching mindfulness meditation and other types of mindfulness training are still evolving. In particular, my basic insight on that clear morning was that college-aged students tended to have very different concerns and interests than many of the adults that entered MBSR training and that the MBSR protocols that I had been studying, while quite effective for adult medical patients or those adults suffering from stress-related illness, did not necessarily address the specific needs of college-aged students. In addition, my research had revealed what I felt like was a hole in the mindfulness literature. While there were many fine books about teaching mindfulness in K-12 classrooms, there were far fewer titles and attention aimed at teaching mindfulness specifically at the university level. And, while there were still many books that explored bringing mindfulness protocols to a college-aged audience in higher education, very few of those books were directly addressed to the college-aged audience, nor did many of them deal directly with concerns germane to that same audience. So, my main creative epiphany that morning, while I walked in silence around the curves of the labyrinth, was that college-aged students could use a text addressed specifically to them, that would introduce a modified form of mindfulness training (not quite as stringent as adult MBSR, yet not quite as simplified as the material being introduced to elementary school children) and contextualize the work around situations and concerns that college-aged students were likely to have. For me, this would be an extension of the work I had done developing a system of meditation training specifically for performing artists by broadening my audience to college-aged emerging adults.

When I returned from that retreat experience, I began to do more research on exactly what was available for mindfulness-based training specifically for college-aged students and found some interesting things. While indeed mindfulness training was starting to proliferate across American campuses, mostly through student mental health organizations, counseling centers, student-led groups, and even some well-organized initiatives (New York University, 2018; University of Southern California, 2018), few universities were yet offering credit-bearing courses on the subject in their course catalogues. The exceptions to this were usually individual college professors, often long-term meditation practitioners themselves, who, working alone, had designed their own class offerings, yet there really was no good textbook available for that kind of class. Most often these individuals would cobble together readings from academic research articles demonstrating the research that now supports the basic concept of mindfulness training and books by Jon Kabat-Zinn, the founder of MBSR. But rarely was there a text that covered both the *practice* of mindfulness and the *movement* to proliferate mindfulness to ever-broadening audiences that might benefit from the practices.

Mindfulness: A Cultural Movement

When I started researching my first book on mindfulness training for performing artists around 2005, the subject was still somewhat obscure and even exotic to the general public. I discuss some of the history of what we call the "mindfulness movement" in Chapter 1 that follows, but in the last dozen years the public awareness of mindfulness practice and the potential benefits to health and individual well-being have exploded. What was a hard topic to discuss with potential publishers in 2005 has now ballooned into a billion-dollar market subset of the alternative health care sector (Wieczner, 2016). In 2005, university programs that offered meditation resources directly to students and faculty were very, very rare. Now a mindfulness program or initiative is commonplace on many university campuses. Research has also grown rapidly in the last several years. Before 2007, there were, on average, fewer than 200 English-language research studies on various forms of meditation and mindfulness practice published annually. However, in 2014, there were 925 such studies published; in 2015 that number reached 1,098; and in 2016, the number of published studies was 1,113 (Goleman & Davidson, 2017, p. 14). From 2000 to 2015, the number of original scientific articles with "mindfulness" or "meditation" in the title, abstract, or keywords grew from less than 100 to more than 32,000. In sum, the interest in scientific research is growing rapidly, as is the industry surrounding the proliferation of mindfulness and meditation practice (Kim, 2018). And with that swelling rise in public and academic interest has come a growth in jobs and potential career paths.

So, in formulating this book, I wanted to not only provide an experiential framework for developing a mindfulness practice (what eventually became CMT, the system introduced in this book), but also an exploration of the mindfulness movement where perhaps many students may want to work in the future. Therefore, as explained in more detail in Chapter 1, this book looks at the subject of mindfulness as both a type of practice and state of consciousness, as well as a socio-cultural movement and emerging industry.

Who This Book Is For

CMT is really aimed at two distinct audiences. It is a hybrid text addressed to both college-aged students and individuals outside of the student context that have an interest in learning about mindfulness as both subject and practice, and professors or instructors interested in a text to support a credit-bearing course on the subject of mindfulness in the university environment. As best as I can determine, at the time of this writing, this is a unique effort combining both practical exercises (praxis) with a didactic exploration of current trends and research to create a textbook *and* a guide for individual exploration depending on the end-user and their particular circumstances. There are certainly many fine books and resources that address mindfulness programs and instruction in higher education (Barbezat & Bush, 2014; Rechtschaffen, 2016; Schonert-Reichl, 2016; Shapiro, Brown, & Astin, 2008; The Center for Contemplative Mind in Society, 2018), but very few of them are addressed at both teachers and students simultaneously. In this respect, I hope that this book will serve a unique purpose.

Students who engage with CMT will find a guide to developing a personal meditation and self-care practice that they can take with them beyond the classroom into their daily lives. Similarly, college-aged emerging adults outside of the university context can use this same text to build a basic meditation practice on their own. The text can be approached in several ways. For those interested in a basic experiential and intellectual grounding in the subject of mindfulness, simply read the text from the beginning, doing the exercises as they are introduced in each chapter (Chapter 8 provides a basic program for implementing these exercises over time to build an individual program of practice), and explore the various subject matters introduced in the text (there is a wealth of supplemental information for deepening this study contained in the various Appendices at the end of this text). For those that really only want to try the experience of meditation practice as an experiment or exploration, perhaps to decide if they can personally benefit or not, you can skim through the informational parts of this book and focus more specifically on just the experiential exercises introduced. Again, Chapter 8 contains a detailed guide about how to use the exercises to build a basic ongoing practice. And finally, perhaps you have already begun meditation in one form or another and are looking for a text to help you expand your explorations or give you some context for experiences you have already had. Hopefully, this text can help you by providing an organized compendium of basic tenets most often fundamental to a secularized meditation practice.

For college-level instructors or teachers of emerging-adult populations in other contexts, this book is both a class text that unfolds in roughly a semester-long format and a useful discussion about how to format or develop a college-level course for either credit or non-credit that will yield a useful and substantive grounding in both praxis and theory surrounding the field and subject of contemporary Western mindfulness practice. Chapter 9 offers a detailed generic model of how a college-level class might be structured, while Appendix A formats the same general content into an example syllabus format that can serve as a basis for customization to the parameters of your own institution or environment. Additionally, there are two other Appendices that will be of interest to the course instructor: a bibliography of additional reading materials and a resource list of numerous organizations and websites where information and support materials can be found.

One other note of importance to those who would endeavor to teach a course of mindfulness in the classroom: As I stress repeatedly in Chapter 9, mindfulness practice is an experiential endeavor. It is therefore critical that anyone who would attempt to teach the practices contained in this book, would first have gained *direct personal experience* though having established an ongoing practice of their own. It is highly recommended that a college-level teacher of CMT have at least one year of experience with a regular meditation practice of some form (which typically does not mean reading about meditation or taking physical yoga classes, but a regular practice of silent meditation of at least 30 minutes per day), or at a bare minimum completion of an eight-week MBSR training and ongoing daily practice. Many instructors that will be attracted to teaching mindfulness at the college level may well have had experience with meditation in the past which is sufficient to justify their qualification to teach CMT, as long as that instructor reacquires and maintains an ongoing practice when teaching. It is also highly recommended that a teacher of CMT is personally involved with an outside teacher or group that can act as their mentor to answer questions and help deepen their personal practice.

What You Will Find in This Book and How to Use It

In general, Chapters 1 through 7 introduce and discuss various subject matters that are either of general interest to the mindfulness student or specifically of interest to the emerging-adult population. Additionally, most chapters include one or more experiential exercises, offered in a progressive order, that, when executed regularly over time, represent a basic mindfulness practice that can be sustained and deepened through continued repetition. The final two chapters are detailed discussions about how to apply the exercises as either an individual practice or in a classroom context as a college instructor. The Appendices represent a large and diverse set of resources for further study and support for either the individual student or instructor.

In Chapter 1 we look at three different definitions of the term "mindfulness." Mindfulness can be explored as a *state of consciousness*, various types of *meditation practice* (including forms of *Focused Attention Meditation*—FAM—and *Open Monitoring Meditation*—OMM), and as a *cultural movement* that has, in particular, been proliferating through the primary and higher education systems in America at accelerating rates for the last decade. We also introduce several experiential exercises that help the reader test their own current powers of attention, explore in a direct way the experience of mindful awareness, and begin to build a repertoire of basic meditation exercises. Additionally, we look at the growing impact that stress, anxiety, and depression are having on the emerging-adult population (college-aged students) and some of the ways an ongoing meditation practice might help.

Chapter 2 looks at some of the research investigating the effects that mobile digital technology and multi-tasking behaviors are having on the attention spans and emotional lives of student-aged populations and heavy-users of technology. The main exercise introduced in this chapter is the *Focused Attention Meditation (FAM) on the Breath* which is a basic meditation form that is widely used around the world. Once the general instructions have been laid out in a guided format (often narrated by the class instructor or through audio recordings), we also explore adding a counting or labeling variation to this fundamental meditation exercise.

Chapter 3 explores a number of contemporary Western forms of secularized meditation that have been used by all kinds of demographics to relieve stress, improve mental concentration, and support general well-being, including the very popular *MBSR Program* (Mindfulness-Based Stress Reduction), *Koru Training* (an introductory program for college-aged students), and *College Mindfulness Training* (CMT), the subject of this book. The experiential exercise in this chapter is *Mindful Movement—Walking*, a new variant on FAM.

Chapter 4 explores ways that mindful awareness can be cultivated outside of formal meditation practices such as have been introduced in previous chapters. This type of mindfulness practice is often called "informal practice" and extends the work into areas such as eating, bathing, and other common daily activities. We also look at some of the experiences that are typically encountered in the early stages of building a mindfulness practice such as "monkey mind" as well as the cumulative and progressive nature of an ongoing mindfulness practice (the effects and benefits tend to grow over time with repetition). We also introduce the concept of the *Silent Retreat* as a way of intensifying and deepening personal practice. Experiential exercises include: *Mindful Eating Exercise #2* (eating an entire meal in a mindful state of awareness), *Mindful Bathing, A Four Hour Silent Mini-Retreat*, and the first formal version of *Open Monitoring Meditation* (OMM), as well as strategies for bringing more awareness to the use of technology and reducing multi-tasking behaviors.

Chapter 5 looks at another approach to both meditation and general self-care that is of potential value to many emerging adults: exercise, nutrition, and fitness training combined with a mindfulness dimension. Research has demonstrated that exercise, diet, and general fitness can be a major factor in physical and psychological well-being and can have particular benefits for the emerging-adult population. We introduce the use of a mantra (repeated word or phrase) as a meditation focal point that is particularly adaptable to combining with physical activity and suggest a way of engaging in exercise that becomes both a workout *and* meditation session. Experiential exercises include: *Seated Mantra Meditation* and the *Mantra-Walking/Jogging Exercise*.

Chapter 6 explores a number of technology platforms that purport to support meditation practice, attentional training, and self-exploration in various ways. Technologies reviewed include the mobile apps *Headspace* and *Calm*, both mobile-digital social media platforms used, in general, as an introduction to meditation practice and each offer a number of features intended to engage the user and keep them progressing toward establishing a long-term practice; *Muse*, which is a wearable EEG monitor that uses real-time brain state information to offer users bio-feedback during the process of meditation practice in an attempt to optimize the focus of attention during the meditation session; *Binaural Beats* and *Brainwave Entrainment Technology*, which are devices that usually combine both light and sound components to encourage relaxation or other optimal brainwave states; and *Flotation Therapy*, which is a type of sensory deprivation technique (originally developed in the middle of the 20th century) that helps focus the mind by reducing sensory input.

Chapter 7 looks at a number of institutionally sponsored mindfulness programs and initiatives, as well as organizations intended to educate and support the proliferation of mindfulness practices in higher education and throughout the broader society. This chapter is useful in understanding various aspects of the mindfulness movement as it exists today and is a useful resource for understanding the kinds of jobs and industry engagements that are emerging in the field of mindfulness studies and the growing commercial market for mindfulness products.

Chapter 8 lays out a format for developing a basic mindfulness practice by the individual working alone or outside of a university class environment utilizing the exercises introduced earlier in the book. It also emphasizes several keep aspects of developing an ongoing practice such as *Goal and Intention Setting* and *Basic Parameters* (requirements and tools) necessary to support an ongoing practice of this nature. The rest of this chapter articulates a model for a beginning program of mindfulness practice that unfolds over a six-month timeframe.

Chapter 9 provides a general outline and discussion for using the material presented in the earlier chapters of this book to develop a semester-long, for-credit course at the college level. The chapter also emphasizes important organizational aspects important to the success of such an endeavor in an institutional setting, including the *CMT Instructor's Personal Practice, Goal and Intention Setting, Basic Programmatic Requirements* (tools or resources) necessary to present a CMT course. A model based on a 16-week semester is then presented as a basis for individual course development that can be customized to various requirements and limitations.

The book concludes with three Appendices. *Appendix A* is a generic syllabus formatted using the outlined material from Chapter 9 as its basis. Individual instructors will be able to use this as a starting point for writing their own syllabi customized to their institution's requirements; not intended as a working model so much as a "jumping-off point" for the creative and motivated teacher. *Appendix B* is a bibliography of additional written resources that may be helpful to the student, researcher, or professor who wants to deepen or extend their knowledge. A careful reading of the material noted in this Appendix will give the reader a very firm grounding in the material underlying the contemporary mindfulness field. *Appendix C* is a simple list of resources, membership organizations, and websites that will be invaluable to the mindfulness professional.

References

Barbezat, D., & Bush, M. (2014). *Contemplative practices in higher education: Powerful methods to transform teaching and learning*. San Francisco: Jossey-Bass.

The Center for Contemplative Mind in Society (2018). The Association for Contemplative Mind in Higher Education website. Retrieved from www.contemplativemind.org/programs/acmhe.

Goleman, D., & Davidson, R.J. (2017). *Altered traits: Science reveals how meditation changes your mind, brain, and body*. New York: Avery.

IMDB (2018). Kevin Page Entry on IMDB.com. Retrieved from www.imdb.com/name/nm0656239.
Kim, H.H. (2018). The meditation industry. *SAGE Business Researcher*. Retrieved from http://businessresearcher.sagepub.com/sbr-1946-105603-2878495/20180129.
New York University (2018). MindfulNYU Web Page. Retrieved from www.nyu.edu/students/communities-and-groups/student-diversity/spiritual-life/mindfulness.html.
Page, K. (2018a). *150% better auditions: Using mindfulness practice to improve your acting*. Dallas: Acting Theory Books, Inc.
Page, K. (2018b). *Advanced consciousness training for actors: Meditation techniques for the performing artist*. New York: Routledge.
Rechtschaffen, D.J. (2016). *The mindful education workbook: Lessons for teaching mindfulness to students* (first edition). New York: W.W. Norton & Company.
Schonert-Reichl, K. (2016). *Handbook of mindfulness in education: Integrating theory and research into practice*. New York: Springer.
Shapiro, S., Brown, K.W, & Astin, J. (2011). Toward the integration of meditation into higher education: A review of research evidence. *Teachers College Record*, *113*(3), 493–528.
University of Southern California (2018). Mindful USC Website. Retrieved from http://mindful.usc.edu/.
Wieczner, J. (2016). Meditating, for love and money. *Fortune*.

1

WHAT EXACTLY IS MINDFULNESS?

The term "mindfulness" has traditionally been difficult to define (Heffernan, 2015). One reason for this is that researchers have often used the term differently in different research studies leading to a difficulty in comparing the results of various studies (Dam et al., 2018). Another reason is that the term can be used interchangeably to describe both states of consciousness ("I am being mindful right now") and different types or styles of meditation practice (Chiesa & Malinowski, 2011). For our purposes, I will use the term mindfulness in three different ways and we will deal with each definition separately.

First, mindfulness can be a way of being in the world or a *state of individual consciousness*. Well-regarded writer and the creator of Mindfulness-Based Stress Reduction therapy (MBSR), Jon Kabat-Zinn, describes this state of consciousness as "paying attention in a particular way: on purpose, in the present moment, and non-judgmentally" (Kabat-Zinn, 2013, p. xxvii). This state of paying attention to what is arising in the present moment of consciousness can be cultivated and trained by using specific meditation techniques that quiet the mind and discipline the attention function of consciousness. This, then, is our second way of using the term mindfulness: as defining a particular *type of meditation practice* that can, when properly engaged over time, cultivate the state of mindful awareness (Lippelt, Hommel, & Colzato, 2014; Valentine & Sweet, 1999). Finally, over the last 20 years, mindfulness has become a *cultural movement* in Western societies that includes the proliferation of numerous approaches to mindfulness practice and mindful consciousness into education (both K-12 and secondary), the workplace, popular culture, psychotherapy, and beyond. The mindfulness movement has spawned books, videos, audio programs, websites, and apps, creating a sub-category of the self-help industry worth over a billion dollars a year, and presumably growing (Wieczner, 2016).

Mindfulness as a State of Consciousness

The ability to focus our attention on events in our environment (which includes internal events such as memories and emotional states) is fundamental to our functioning as human beings. Without the ability to selectively direct and focus attention, we would not long survive in the world. However, many people are surprised when they test their own abilities of attentional focus at how easily distracted they become. Try the following experiential exercise. Read the instructions and *have the experience* before reading on to the next section. (Reprinted from *Advanced Consciousness Training for Actors* by Kevin Page, 2018, with permission from Routledge Press.)

THE WATCH EXERCISE

Locate a watch with a *second hand* or a clock on the wall. A traditional mechanical stopwatch is best. Please avoid digital readouts (i.e., clocks with numbers). If you only have a smartphone, download a stopwatch program that allows you to view a traditional clock face with a functioning second hand. The problem with digital readouts is that they require you to conceptualize "numbers" instead of following the progress of the second hand as it makes its way around in a simple circle. Using a second hand will make this exercise *much* simpler. If you have no other options, the exercise can be attempted with a digital readout, but the results may vary substantially.

Sit either in a chair or on the floor, so that you will be comfortable and without distraction for at least five minutes. Either start the timing function on the stopwatch or pick a time on the watch/clock face to begin the exercise.

Concentrate your attention on the second hand of the clock and think about nothing else for five minutes. Neither remove your eyes from the clock face nor become distracted in any way. If you find that your thoughts have wandered to anything but the clock's second hand, you have failed the exercise and must start over. Begin ...

How did you do?

If you made it past a minute, you did better than most people that have not had specific attentional training. This exercise is intended to highlight the difficulties and challenges of focusing the untrained attentional function within your own consciousness. Now let us try an exercise that comes at the issue from a different angle by highlighting what the experience of "paying attention on purpose, in the present moment, and non-judgmentally" actually feels like.

One of the most common activities of human beings is eating. In most cases, it is something we do several times a day and often under a variety of circumstances. In many cases, eating is done habitually with little awareness dedicated to the act or the sensations of the act beyond meeting the overriding goal of quenching physical hunger. While an exquisite or special-occasion meal may merit careful attention to the various flavors, smells, and other pleasures of eating, most often, particularly in Western culture, we plow through our meals with little actual consciousness of the experience.

A favorite early exercise in many MBSR trainings is called "the raisin-eating exercise," which brilliantly plays off of our general inattentiveness to our eating habits in order to introduce the basic idea of mindfulness practice (Kabat-Zinn, 2013, pp. 15–16). Below, I will offer my own adaptation of an eating exercise that can be used to generate an immediately observable sensation of present moment attentional focus (or mindfulness). This exercise can be done in a group setting where the instructor or facilitator guides the process by narrating the instructions, or it can be done individually by simply following the instructions below.

MINDFUL EATING EXERCISE #1

Instructions:

Take a single piece of a small fruit or other bite-sized, hand-held food item (such as a raisin, grape, piece of candy, peanut or shelled pecan-half, pretzel, or cracker, etc.) Sit comfortably but erect in a chair. If you normally slouch, you might consider sitting on the front edge of the chair with your body aligned and your back relatively straight. The idea is to be comfortable but alert throughout the experience without the need to shift or change positions often, so that the focus can remain on the activity.

Take a few moments to settle into your seat and become present to the moment. You might bring your attention to your breath for a few cycles.

Observe the food object in your hand. Pay complete attention to it. Explore its qualities carefully. Look at the object as if you have never seen such a thing before. Hold the object up near your face and view it from all angles, turning it around between your fingers. Track the movement of your arm as it raises the object in front of your eyes, what muscles are you using to accomplish this? What are the sensations of your fingertips as you turn the object around? Squeeze the object and experience its consistency and weight. What does it look like when held up to the light? Is it translucent? Are there patterns on its surface? Does it make any sounds when turned or squeezed between the fingers near the ear? Investigate the object in any ways you can think of (but do not put it in your mouth ... yet) and also note any kinesthetic or emotional reactions you might have. Is the object pleasant or subtly repulsive? Take at least a minute to explore the object thoroughly. Be creative with your investigation.

Raise the object to your lips, but do *not* put it directly into your mouth. What was the sensation of simply rubbing the small food object against your lips? Is there any reaction in your body? Do you start to salivate?

> Slowly place the object in your mouth and just hold it on your tongue for a full minute, exploring the sensations that go along with having food in your mouth but not chewing. You may suck it gently and explore any faint flavors that might arise. Move the object around in your mouth, still without biting into it, and experience the texture against your tongue, teeth, and gums. Do you salivate? Do any emotions or memories arise? Just take in what experience is there in the moment.
>
> Finally, you are invited to bite into the food object and chew it in a wholly controlled and deliberate manner, noting each sensation and flavor as it arises in consciousness, discovering as if for the first time the experience of chewing and swallowing.

How was this experience for you? Were you able to stay with the sensations of eating in this manner? Did you find it easier to stay focused on this activity than to simply follow a clock's second hand as in the previous exercise? Were you present to the sensations as they occurred? Did you observe anything new about the eating process or discover a previously unrecognized quality of the food object that you used? In other words, were you more mindful of the actions and experiences that arose in your consciousness as you performed the exercise than you normally would be? This is the experience of mindfulness as a *state of consciousness*.

Most people find this experience fairly easy to grasp when presented in a form like the mindful eating exercise, yet more difficult to achieve when approached through the watch exercise. Why is that? The reason is that a state of mindfulness is very simple, it really is nothing more than paying "bare attention" to the experiences of the present moment, as Kabat-Zinn suggests, but the ability to do so at will often requires training. Which brings us to our next perspective on the term mindfulness, which is mindfulness as a particular type of meditation practice.

Mindfulness as a Type of Meditation

Meditation as a mental practice has been around for at least 3,500 years of human history (Everly & Lating, 2002, p. 199). Meditation can take many forms and have various effects depending on a number of factors, including the individual's predispositions and developmental state; intentions for engaging in the practice; the setting, circumstances, and guidance of the practice; and length of time and intensity of engagement. As an example, the noticeable effects of a meditation practice that is taken on casually for 30 minutes a day, three days a week, as part of a university class that has as its goal the reduction of student stress, may vary significantly from the effects of a serious meditation practice taken on as a spiritual discipline with the intention of achieving a permanent state of self-realization under the tutelage of a master meditation teacher for periods of three to six hours a day for a year of sequestered living in a remote monastery. The differences in level of commitment and intention in the foregoing examples are obvious and the precipitate effects would no doubt vary widely.

For our purposes, we will be looking at various meditation practices and techniques that fall along a very narrow spectrum of the entire field of possibilities, with the intention of positively impacting the student's sense of well-being and performance in their existing circumstances, presumably some type of academic pursuit and young adult developmental tasks. The exercises we will explore are intentionally rudimentary and curated specifically for a college-aged demographic. We will be looking at the meditation process primarily through a Western scientific lens as well as a first-person hermeneutic (interpretive) exploration of direct experience. For the student or explorer that wishes to go further, there is a good deal of literature available (see Appendix B at the end of this volume for many examples), and the instruction of an experienced teacher is highly recommended. What will be suggested in the following pages is intended to be helpful to its audience, but not necessarily transformative (which has traditionally oft been the goal of engaging in a serious meditative practice). There is much to be had from a beginner's approach. In the practice of Zen, as an example, the practitioner is asked to cultivate a "beginner's mind," and so shall we proceed with a secular intent and an innocent curiosity.

Often in Western meditation research, two general types of practice are identified, "Focused Attention Meditation" (FAM), sometimes called *concentration meditation* or meditation with an object, and "Open Monitoring Meditation" (OMM), or *meditation upon conscious experience* itself (Lippelt et al., 2014; Lutz, Slagter, Dunne, & Davidson, 2008). In FAM, practitioners attempt to focus their attention on a single object, such as the process of their own breathing or a mantra (a repeated word or phrase) and maintain attention on that object for the duration of the meditation session. When other thoughts or distractions inevitably encroach on the concentration of attention, the meditators are instructed to gently acknowledge the thought or distraction and then, non-judgmentally, return their attention to the object of the meditation session. The practice of gently holding the attention on a single object and the act of repeatedly returning the attention to the object when attention wanders off, work together over time to train and strengthen the attention function and result in a more stable state of consciousness that can be more readily directed at will. While the basic instructions for FAM appear exceedingly simple (and they are) the actual practice performed on a regular basis over time can be challenging for many and exceptionally difficult for some, depending on how generally distracted and distractible they tend to be.

OMM has a slightly different focus and is often taken up after basic competency in FAM has been achieved (Chiesa & Malinowski, 2011; Lippelt et al., 2014). In OMM, the focus of attention is on whatever experience is arising in consciousness at the moment. Instead of focusing on one object and ignoring all other phenomena, the meditator endeavors to "gently" be aware of everything arising in consciousness without judgment or attachment. Attention is left open to experience whatever is present—sounds in the room, thoughts and memories, the sensation of the space around the meditator—whatever is happening now is accepted and acknowledged (very much like in the eating exercise above). This is open awareness or what is sometimes called cultivating a state of bare attention, so that the meditator's awareness receives and accepts whatever arises in the present moment.

FAM and OMM can both be used as the foundation for various meditative forms, such as seated meditation, walking meditation, movement meditation, or meditative versions of such everyday tasks as eating or bathing. We will look at examples of both in our explorations, but as suggested above, we will start with forms based on FAM in order to build some expertise in directing the attention function before moving on to forms based on OMM.

A meditation (or mindfulness) practice then is made up of a combination of exercises and disciplines based on either concentrating the attention repeatedly on a single object or process, or attending carefully (and non-judgmentally) to all experiences that arise in consciousness on a real-time, or present-moment, basis. By repeatedly and regularly training the attention to return to specific objects or overall awareness of experience, we begin to calm the otherwise active puppy dog mind and this, in turn, can lead to greater relaxation, equanimity, and clarity of mind even under difficult circumstances, the general goals of our program of college mindfulness training.

The Mindfulness Movement in the 21st Century

In the last 20 years, mindfulness in particular, and meditation in general, has become a cultural movement in the United States. However, this wave of popularization and resulting proliferation is a relatively recent turn of events. In the 1800s and early 1900s, meditation and yoga were generally categorized along with occult practices and beliefs. Westerners tended to look on such practices as mysterious and exotic or with magical and perhaps anti-Christian overtones. In 1920, an Indian master yoga teacher, Yogananda (born Mukunda Lal Ghosh, 1893–1952) came to America on a quest to spread the practice of Kriya Yoga and its attendant meditation techniques to a Western audience. He lectured widely under the title of Swami Yogananda Giri (Yogananda, 2007, p. 305). In 1946 he published the story of his life, *The Autobiography of a Yogi*, which became widely read and was one of the first books available in English on Eastern spiritual/mystical philosophy to receive broad distribution.

During the cultural revolution of the 1960s, a general interest in contemplative practices began to emerge throughout the broader culture, this included the human potential movement and the explosion of interest in what became known as alternative or New Age spirituality. Due to the Chinese invasion of Tibet and years of war across Southeast Asia, many monks and advanced teachers of meditation practice began to emigrate to the United States and Europe, bringing their teachings with them. During the 1960s another Hindu-influenced guru began teaching a form of Vedic mantra-based meditation that he called Transcendental Meditation or "TM," to a number of Western pop cultural figures, including the rock group The Beatles (Gilpin, 2006; Goldberg, 2010). In 1971, a former Harvard professor, who had been involved with psychedelic research, went to India on a personal spiritual quest, and when he returned changed his name from Richard Alpert to Ram Dass and published a book titled *Be Here Now* (Ram & Lama Foundation, 1971), which became tremendously popular within the American hippy movement. However, the scientific establishment remained skeptical of the value of such practices primarily due to their subjective and introspective qualities. Consciousness researcher, Charles T. Tart, published a book entitled *Altered States of Consciousness* in 1969, and claimed that at that time there were only three scientifically controlled studies on meditation available in Western academic journals (Page, 2006). That condition, however, was soon to change.

In 1979, a Western molecular biologist and meditator in the Buddhist tradition named Jon Kabat-Zinn convinced the Department of Ambulatory Care at the University of Massachusetts Medical Center Hospital to host a clinic that would teach a secularized version of traditional Buddhist meditation practices to medical patients that were experiencing chronic pain and stress-related disorders. He called his particular version of meditation training Mindfulness-Based Stress Reduction (MBSR) and developed it using language and descriptions he hoped would be accepted by the medical community, which at that time still held a powerfully negative bias toward meditation practice and much of what we would call today alternative or integrative medicine (Kabat-Zinn, 2013, pp. 170–171). MBSR became both successful and popular and as of the present time Kabat-Zinn's UMass program has trained more than 24,000 people in its meditation-based stress reduction techniques, along with over 1,000 certified MBSR instructors and spawned MBSR programs in more than 700 medical settings in more than 30 countries. Perhaps more importantly, the MBSR program, along with many other efforts by individual scientists, medical doctors, and psychologists, has ignited an explosion in scientifically based research projects on the benefits and outcomes of meditation practices, often under controlled, laboratory conditions. Since the late 1960s when Charles Tart made his observations about the dearth of empirical research, the number of papers published in Western medical and psychological journals has grown exponentially. A recent survey counted 6,838 such papers (quite a growth spike from 1969's three). The number of papers on the topic of meditation and its related concepts published in 2014 alone totaled 925; in 2015, that number grew to 1,098; and in 2016 the total was 1,113 such publications in English-language scientific literature (Goleman & Davidson, 2017).

It would appear that meditation, which includes the concepts we have been discussing under the general term mindfulness, has become a mainstream interest. Serious applications, called mindfulness-based interventions (MBIs) have been adapted for and delivered to populations with disorders that include cancer, heart disease, diabetes, brain injuries, fibromyalgia, HIV/Aids, Parkinson's, organ transplants, psoriasis, irritable bowel syndrome, and tinnitus. Mindfulness has become common in the mental health profession and is regularly used in the treatment of attention-deficit hyperactivity disorder, depression, anxiety, obsessive-compulsive disorder, personality disorders, substance abuse, and autism. There are now hundreds of programs to deploy various mindfulness-type exercises in K-12 schools across the country. In 2016, *Time* magazine dedicated an entire issue, later published as a special edition, on the subject of mindfulness in our contemporary culture (The Editors of *Time*, 2016). Several major corporations have made mindfulness training available to their managers and employees.

Part of the purpose of this book is to help prepare students from the medical, psychological, teaching, and other helping professions, as well as those with a general interest, for the jobs and programs that will continue to emerge out of the broader mindfulness and meditation movements as they grow. While this book will not fully prepare you to teach mindfulness as such—for that you will need direct, hands-on training with a qualified teacher to oversee your own experiential work—it will give you a grounding in both the basics of those experiential practices and a solid academic introduction to the various aspects of what we might call the emerging mindfulness field.

Emerging Adulthood and College Stress

The college years and the college experience can be a time of high stress. In a 2016 survey that included 95,761 students at 137 US post-secondary schools, sponsored by the American College Health Association (ACHA), 49.8% of all students had "felt things were hopeless" at some point in the last 12 months; 85.1% of all students had "felt overwhelmed by all they had to do" at some point in the last 12 months; 81.7% of all students had "felt exhausted—not from physical activity" at some point in the last 12 months; 58.4% of all students had "felt overwhelming anxiety" at some point in the last 12 months; and 36.7% of all students had "felt so depressed that it was difficult to function" at some point in the last 12 months.

In another report from student mental health providers, sponsored by the Center for Collegiate Mental Health (CCMH), consisting of data from 139 university and college counseling centers covering over 100,000 students that had sought out counseling services during the 2014–2015 academic year, as well as trends identified from data collected from 2010 through 2015, researchers found the growth in the number of students seeking services at counseling centers (+29.6%) was more than five times the rate of institutional enrollment (+5.6%).

The 2015 report concluded that "three types of self-reported distress have demonstrated slow but consistent growth over [a five-year period] including: Depression, Anxiety, and Social Anxiety … these specific areas parallel the most common presenting concerns, Depression and Anxiety, as determined by clinicians" (Center for Collegiate Mental Health, 2015). In the 2016 edition of this same report, the researchers further emphasized:

> Anxiety and depression continue to be the most common presenting concerns for college students as identified by counseling center staff. In addition, students' self-reported distress levels for depression, generalized anxiety, and social anxiety continue to evidence slight but persistent increases each year for the past six years.
>
> *(Center for Collegiate Mental Health, 2016)*

However, in yet another study of stress in the college population, researchers looked at the perceptions of stress by college students and the perceptions of student stress by faculty members at the same institutions and found a significant variance in which the faculty perceived higher levels and more incidence of stress reactions in the students than the students themselves actually perceived or reported (Misra, McKean, West, & Russo, 2000). Such results point to the fact that, while stress (and particularly incidents of excessive stress) may be a salient theme in higher education populations, the actual occurrences of, and negative effects from, are still a very individual affair. And so, from the perspective of this book, while generally acknowledging the potential for excessive or negative stress reactions in a collegiate environment, the student is cautioned to examine their own personal situation carefully and attempt an accurate self-evaluation of their unique "stress reaction profile."

So, what are some of the top reasons that students who do experience significant levels of stress in college report as their major stressors or stress triggers? I asked a number of college counselors (as well as meditation teachers that offer services to this demographic) what their students most often reported, and the majority of answers seemed to cluster around academic performance and competition, interpersonal (often romantic) relationships, and uncertainty about the future. Interestingly, these three general areas corollate nicely with the areas identified as of highest concern to "emerging adults" (18–25 years of age), by researcher Jeffery Arnett in his studies of the emerging-adult developmental stage (Arnett, 2000). Arnett has theorized that a new, previously unidentified developmental stage has emerged in America and other developed countries that falls between the traditional stages of adolescence and young adulthood, called emerging adulthood, which is characterized by identity explorations in these three general areas: work, love, and worldviews. It would appear that when college-aged students feel high levels of stress, it often centers around these same general areas of concern that Arnett identified for the emerging adult.

In the 2016 Center for Collegiate Mental Health report mentioned earlier, the top three conditions presented by students at university counseling centers as reasons for treatment were: anxiety (61%), depression (49%), and stress (45.3%). Interestingly, meditation training and other MBIs have been developed and adapted as treatments for each of these conditions. Mindfulness-Based Cognitive Therapy (MBCT) is widely used in the treatment of depression and depression relapse prevention (Segal, Williams, & Teasdale, 2013), and MBSR (which we will discuss more fully in Chapter 3) is a popular prescription for adult patients with stress and anxiety disorders in medical contexts (Kabat-Zinn, 2013).

With so much potential for stress and stressful situations in the collegiate environment and given the primary concerns of the emerging-adult populations of these institutions, it is fairly easy to see that stress and anxiety-related reactions could be a major impediment to academic performance and learning. In yet another study entitled *Mindfulness Training Improves Working Memory Capacity and GRE Performance while Reducing Mind Wandering* (Mrazek, Franklin, Phillips, Baird, & Schooler, 2013), researchers looked at the effects of two weeks' worth of meditation training (45 minute sessions, four times a week) on emerging adults before taking the Graduate Records Exam (GRE). They found notable improvements in both "GRE reading-comprehension scores and working memory capacity while simultaneously reducing the occurrence of distracting thoughts during completion of the GRE" (Mrazek et al., 2013, p. 776).

With this evidence in hand, let us now look at some practical applications of meditation and mindfulness training that might be useful in a university or collegiate context.

Relieving Stress and Focusing the Mind

Holly Rogers, co-creator of the KORU Mindfulness Program, that we will discuss at length in Chapter 3, recommends introducing emerging-adult students to simple stress reduction techniques (as well as introductory meditation practices) at the very beginning of any mindfulness-based training to give the students practical and useful exercises that they can apply in their lives with immediate positive results (Rogers, 2018). Given the likelihood that college-aged students may be experiencing various levels of elevated stress, this seems like an excellent strategy for beginning our college mindfulness training process.

Conscious Breathing

The following exercise, that I call simply Conscious Breathing, is an adaptation of both Shibashi and BaDuanJin Qigong, a traditional Chinese movement meditation/exercise sequence based on T'ai Chi Ch'uan practice and philosophy. What will be presented below is *derived* from the opening movements of a variety of

Qigong styles. What I am presenting here is specifically intended as a form of conscious breathing exercise to calm the nerves, focus the attention, and immediately reduce stress, and, as such, should not be mistaken for formal Qigong instruction, which can be acquired successfully from other sources.

In this breathing/movement exercise, we are concentrating on the flow of physical movements in concert with our natural breathing pattern. The speed of the exercise will generally be guided by your natural breathing rhythm, which may change from session to session. In the guided script below, I will utilize a number of metaphors describing "subtle energies" in the body. These metaphors are not intended to be taken literally so much as provide a set of internalized images with which to direct the attention.

Below is a script that can be used for group practice in the initial sessions to learn the sequence. It can easily be adapted to individual use if you are working alone. The script can be read aloud by a group leader or the course instructor, or it can be pre-recorded for playback during practice sessions. When the pattern of this simple exercise has been learned, the recorded guidance or narration can be dropped, and the movements can be internally self-directed. Once mastered, the Conscious Breathing exercise can be used almost any time as an immediate and effective stress reduction technique and as a warm-up or quick attention-focusing exercise.

CONSCIOUS BREATHING

Instructions:

It is best if cellphones or digital devices are turned off during this exercise to minimize distraction (even a muted vibrating alert from a cellphone is a distraction from this kind of concentration-of-attention work).

All movement exercises are generally best approached wearing loose, comfortable clothing or athletic wear when possible. Where appropriate, this exercise can be done in bare or stocking feet. A direct connection between the feet and the surface of the ground can be useful but is not absolutely necessary.

This sequence can be practiced inside or outside, but it is often best at the beginning to practice in a quiet and secure inside location where distractions and interruptions can be minimized, and everyone involved can clearly hear the instructions.

All participants should find a space where they can move freely and not interfere or intersect with any other participant's movements. As with all focused attention practices, the focus is primarily internal.

This exercise is done at the pace of your natural breathing cycle. So, in the sequences between guidance and narration of the movements, make sure to attend to your own body and its rhythms, following the pace of *your* breath and not necessarily the movements of others in the room.

Guidance Script:
Conscious breathing begins by standing comfortably in an aligned position.

Take a position where your feet are shoulder-width apart and settle into your chosen spot. Close your eyes for a moment. (Pause.)

Become aware of your body in space. Notice how your body is balanced on this very spot. Feel your feet in contact with the floor. Relax your body. Stand in alignment, feet relaxed but firmly planted, knees unlocked and slightly bent, pelvis tucked slightly under your torso, spine erect and arms loose at your sides, your elbows slightly bent, hands relaxed and fingers slightly curled. You may want to gently roll your shoulders a couple of times, allowing the chest to open as you settle into a relaxed, aligned position.

Now, imagine a string coming out of the top of your head, a balloon attached at the end, gently pulling your whole body upwards from the crown of your head, helping you float, spine straight, lengthening, relaxed. (Pause.)

Still with your eyes closed, sense your body on this spot, in relation to gravity, any small movements or swaying that may take place. Take it all in, the sensations of the body as you simply stand here, in this moment, erect but relaxed. (Pause.)

And now, let your attention move to your breath. Feel the sensation of coolness at the tips of your nostrils as the breath enters your body and travels through your lungs. Feel the belly rising as the breath fills your body and the chest expands, and now a pause ... before exhalation begins and the process is reversed. Just be with the breath as you stand here, in this moment, centered and calm and relaxed. Fully experience *this* breath ... and *this* breath ... and *this* breath. (Pause.)

Now you may open your eyes. Gaze with a soft focus in front of you without focusing on one particular spot or object. Just let your eyes relax and rest where they fall.

As your next inhalation begins, allow your arms to float up in front of you to shoulder-height, palms down toward the floor. The wrists remain relaxed and the hands soft. Imagine gentle rays of energy pouring from your chest, down your arms and through your fingers, radiating to the horizon. As the exhalation begins, let your wrists relax, hands almost floating at the ends of your arms like air-filled balloons, and allow your arms to gently fall back to your sides in rhythm with your exhalation, palms ending facing your thighs, fingers relaxed.

With the next in-breath, the arms float up in front of you to shoulder height ... and again float down to your sides as the breath naturally releases from your body. Continue raising and lowering your arms to the natural rhythm of your breath for the next several cycles, staying present to the experience, savoring the sensations of each unique breath and each unique movement and flow of your arms as they float up ... and back ... up ... and back. (Pause.)

[Participants keep performing the movements for between six and ten breath cycles.]

Now when your arms return to your sides this time, relax into a standing meditation pose again. Notice how your body is balanced on this very spot. Feel your feet in contact with the floor. Stand in alignment, feet relaxed but firmly planted, check to see that your knees are unlocked and slightly bent, pelvis tucked slightly under your torso, spine erect and arms loose at your sides, palms facing your thighs, elbows slightly bent, hands relaxed and fingers slightly curled. (Pause.)

[Participants continue breathing.]

And now, beginning with your next inhalation, allow your arms to float up in front of you to shoulder-height, palms facing down toward the floor. The wrists remain relaxed and the hands soft. On the exhale, turn your palms facing each other and open the arms out to the sides, keeping the elbows slightly bent, so that by the end of your exhalation, your arms are spread wide at your sides, shoulder height, as if you were inviting a huge hug from a friend or family member. Now, with your next in-breath, close the circle of your arms, bringing them back to front, shoulder height once more, and turn the palms down, facing the floor so that you finish the inhale with your arms extended in front of you as before. Finally, as the exhale begins, let your wrists relax, hands almost floating at the ends of your arms like air-filled balloons, and allow your arms to gently fall back to your sides in rhythm with your exhalation, palms ending facing your thighs, fingers relaxed.

Continue this sequence for the next several breath cycles at the natural pace of your own breathing. (Pause.)

[Participants keep performing the movements for between six and ten breath cycles.]

And as you complete this cycle of breath and movement, relax into standing meditation pose once more. Notice how your body is balanced on this very spot. Feel your feet in contact with the floor. Stand in alignment, feet relaxed but firmly planted; check to see that your knees are unlocked and slightly bent, pelvis tucked slightly under your torso, spine erect and arms loose at your sides, palms facing your thighs, elbows slightly bent, hands relaxed and fingers slightly curled ... and tune into your breathing once again. (Pause.)

[Participants continue breathing.]

And now, beginning with your next inhalation, bring your hands together in front of your pelvis, middle fingertips touching, palms now toward the ceiling; and as the breath enters, scoop up the energy from your lower body, raising your hands up to chest height, keeping them near the body with the inhalation. As you begin to exhale, turn the palms down and intertwine your fingers, pressing your laced hands back down toward the ground, running them closely down the front of your body and stretching your arms as you extend and the exhalation finishes.

With the next inhale, repeat the process by untwining the fingers and switching the palms up again toward the ceiling, middle fingertips touching and keeping the hands near the front of the body. Scoop up the energy with your hands so that they end, once again, at chest height. As the exhale begins, turn the palms down and intertwine your fingers, pressing your laced hands back down toward the ground, this time out from your body at a 45-degree angle toward the floor, stretching your arms as you extend and the exhalation finishes.

With the next inhalation, release your fingers and return your hands to the front of the pelvis, middle fingertips touching, scoop up the energy with your hands so that they end, once again, at chest height, near the body. As the exhale begins, once again intertwine your fingers, this time pressing straight out from your chest, arms parallel to the ground, stretching your arms as you extend and the exhalation finishes.

Let the arms fall to the front of your pelvis, and with the next inhalation, repeat the scooping motion in front of the body and to chest height with the palms up toward the ceiling. This time, as the exhalation begins, turn the palms out and intertwine your fingers as you press out and up 45 degrees from center so that your arms extend out and just over your head, stretching your arms as you extend and the exhalation finishes.

As the final inhale of the sequence begins, the hands float down in front of the pelvis and the scooping of energy across the front of the body is repeated once more. As the exhale begins, the fingers interlace, and the palms extend out and up toward the ceiling, stretching through the arms and sending the energy scooped up from the lower body up to the sky. As the arms stretch at the end of the movement, rise up onto the toes so that your intertwined hands are stretching the whole length of your body from your arms down to your toes. Release the hands and let them float down to the starting position in front of your pelvis, once more with palms facing upward and middle fingertips touching.

With the next inhalation, begin the sequence again, this time at the natural pace of your own breath. Repeat the full sequence: up-and-down, up-and-out at 45 degrees, up-and-out from the chest, up-and-out 45 degrees above center, and up-and-out above the head, always returning to scoop up the energy of the lower body with the inhalation of each new breath.

Repeat the sequence six times at your own pace, maintaining constant awareness of each movement and each breath in the moment that it happens. If you find that your mind has wandered during the sequence, gently but firmly return it to the natural flow of your movements and breath. (Pause.)

[Participants keep performing the movements until they complete their individual sequences.]

When you complete your final sequence, let your hands float freely to your sides and relax into standing meditation pose once more. Notice how your body is balanced on this very spot. Feel your feet in contact with the floor.

> Stand in alignment, feet relaxed but firmly planted; check to see that your knees are unlocked and slightly bent, pelvis tucked slightly under your torso, spine erect and arms loose at your sides, palms facing your thighs, elbows slightly bent, hands relaxed and fingers slightly curled ... and tune into your breathing once again. (Pause.)
>
> When you are ready, slowly and gently, while still maintaining an awareness of your breath, allow your awareness to expand to include the room around you, the activity in the space, and the presence of your friends.

This exercise may take several repetitions through the guided version for participants to master the simple flowing movements; but once it is internalized, conscious breathing is an excellent warm-up exercise to start the day as well as calm the nerves at any time when stress levels become excessive or uncomfortable.

The Traditional Body Scan

The first meditation practice usually introduced in MBSR training, a program we will investigate more closely in a later chapter, is called *the body scan*. It is a form of concentration or FAM practice, discussed earlier, and it typically takes between half an hour and 45 minutes to complete, making it one of the longer exercises we will investigate in this book. It is considered a form of FAM because the exercise consists of a series of directions to focus the attention on specific parts of the body while simultaneously relaxing the areas of the body receiving the attention.

The traditional body scan meditation has several features that make it a good introductory exercise. First, it uses parts of the body as the focal object of attention, making the experience of concentrating on an object very immediate and felt (as in sensations). It can be easier for beginners to focus and maintain their attention on concrete sensations, such as in the hands or feet, than on the more complex and evolving sensations involved in the process of breathing, for instance (which we will get to in the next chapter). Also, the body scan is a deeply, kinesthetically relaxing exercise and is perceived as pleasant and desirable by most beginning students once they learn how it is done. The body scan often produces drowsiness, as it is most often done lying down with eyes either closed or softly focused and can be used as a method for getting to sleep at night once the technique is mastered. (However, the initial goal is to stay awake and alert throughout the sequence.)

As with conscious breathing presented above, the following script is written for a group leader or instructor to read aloud during the practice and can be used as either a group or individual exercise. The script can also be pre-recorded and played back to guide the exercise. However, once again, once the basic instructions have been learned, the traditional body scan can be internally self-directed and used in almost any scenario where relative quiet and safety are available. (I, for instance, will often use a short version of the body scan while traveling through airports or waiting in lobbies as a way to refresh my energy and focus my attention.)

> ### THE TRADITIONAL BODY SCAN
>
> Instructions:
>
> No cellphones or digital devices should be present in the room during this exercise, even vibration alerts are distracting. So, power the devices completely off and put them away, out of sight, before the session begins.
>
> Once you've found your position, settle in and allow your awareness to turn inward.
>
> Lie on the floor for this exercise. You may want to use a yoga mat and some low pillows to support your neck and slightly raise the knees. Place your hands comfortably at your sides, either palms up or down. Hands can also be draped lightly on top of your abdomen but avoid interlocking the fingers. The goal is to remain comfortably in this position for half an hour or more without the need to overly shift or adjust your position. Relaxation will be an integral part of this exercise. The body scan can also be done in a seated position, but remember to keep the back fairly straight and neither slouch nor sit rigidly tense; again the idea is to find a position where the body is naturally aligned but relaxed and comfortable enough to maintain the position without strain or fidgeting.
>
> While you can close your eyes, I often recommend keeping them open and softly focused. If you are seated, you can let your eyelids droop slightly and pick a spot on the floor between three and five feet in front of you, where you can focus without straining. Again, you want a soft focus so that while individual objects may be slightly blurred, you are still able to see the objects in your immediate field of vision. If you are lying down, pick an area of the ceiling (or sky) that you can gaze upon easily, again, without staring. The point is to *stay awake and alert* for the duration of the exercise without falling asleep or causing tension in the eyes. If you choose to close your eyes, be warned that this often can lead to sleep, which is not our goal; and so, if you find yourself drifting out of consciousness, you may want to open your eyes, blink a few times, and maintain a soft focus as you continue. If you do fall asleep, however, do not judge or criticize yourself unduly. Falling asleep is actually very common during the learning phase of this work, and so treat yourself with kindness and try to stay awake the next time you do the exercise.
>
> Unless you otherwise cannot, due to blocked airways or the like, it is recommended that you keep your mouth closed during all meditation exercises and *breathe through your nose*. While your mouth is closed, allow your tongue to rest, pressed gently against the front teeth. This will prevent excessive salivation and swallowing, which can be a distraction during an extended session.

Guidance Script:

Take a moment to settle into the body. Release any tensions and allow awareness to focus on the breathing.

Simply experience the body breathing for the next five breaths. (Pause.)

Noticing the breath, continue releasing any tensions as attention turns inward.

Imagining the body as a balloon filled with nothing but air. Light, nearly weightless. The body floating on a cloud of warm relaxation.

The breath enters the nose and travels through the chest cavity, down into the abdomen. With each new breath, the belly fills with air, the chest rises, there is a pause, and then the sensation of exhaling. The chest lowers, the abdomen contracts in the reverse order of the inhalation. Just sitting (or lying) with those sensations for a moment; the body light as a balloon, the torso filling with air for every breath-cycle. (Pause.)

With the next inhalation, allowing the breath to travel in through the nose, it flows down the left side of the body, along the left leg, and makes its way to the left foot. The breath flows, with the attention, through the body, and gently settles in the left foot. As the breathing continues, the attention finally settles in the left big toe. For the next few breath cycles, only the left big toe exists. (Pause.)

And now, with the next breath, the attention expands to take in the other toes of the left foot; sensing each toe in order; sensing the skin between each toe; breathing into the toes and allowing them to relax. Everything is light, filled with nothing but air. (Pause.)

Now the attention flows down to the ball of the foot. Breathing into the ball of the foot and releasing any tension there. (Pause.)

The attention moves to the blade and the arch of the left foot. Perhaps the sensations are different on one side of the foot than the other? The attention caresses the foot.

The attention moves into the heel of the left foot; the back of the ankle, where the Achilles tendon connects to the heel; all as light as a balloon; all filled with nothing but air. (Pause.)

The attention moves to the top of the left foot; flowing from the top of the foot, around the bottom, and back to the top. And now the attention widens to take in the entire foot all at once; the breath filling the foot like a weightless balloon. (Pause.)

With the next breath, the attention flows up to the left calf, releasing any tension there might be there. Experience just the calf for a moment. The back of the calf. The front of the shin. Just breathe and be with the whole of the left calf for a moment.

And now, the attention moves up to the left knee. The breath fills the left knee. The top of the kneecap, the back of the knee; the whole knee becomes a balloon. (Pause.)

With the next breath, the attention moves up to the left thigh. The top of the thigh, from the knee up to the hip. Each breath fills the thigh with air, nearly weightless, like a balloon floating on the breeze. Now, the attention flows to the back of the thigh, along the hamstring, and up to the buttock with each new breath. (Pause.)

And now the attention moves into the pelvis. The breath fills the pelvis. Feel the connection the back of the pelvis makes with the chair or the floor. The pelvic area relaxes as it fills with breath on every inhale, and releases with every exhale.

With the next breath, the attention flows down the right leg and into the right foot. As with the left foot, the attention comes to rest in the right big toe. In this moment, there is nothing but the right big toe.

And now, with the next breath, the attention expands to take in the other toes of the right foot; sensing each toe in order; the skin between each toe; breathing into the toes and allowing them to relax. Everything is light, filled with nothing but air. (Pause.)

Now the attention flows down to the ball of the foot. Breathing into the ball of the foot and releasing any tension there. (Pause.)

The attention moves to the blade and the arch of the right foot. Perhaps the sensations are different on one side of the foot than the other? The attention caresses the foot.

The attention moves into the heel of the right foot; the back of the ankle, where the Achilles tendon connects to the heel; all as light as a balloon; all filled with nothing but air. (Pause.)

The attention moves to the top of the right foot; flowing from the top of the foot, around the bottom, and back to the top. And now the attention widens to take in the entire foot all at once; the breath filling the foot like a weightless balloon. (Pause.)

With the next breath, the attention flows up to the right calf, releasing any tension there might be there. Experience just the calf for a moment. The back of the calf. The front of the shin. Just breathe and be with the whole of the right calf for a moment.

And now, the attention moves up to the right knee. The breath fills the right knee. The top of the kneecap, the back of the knee; the whole knee becomes a balloon. (Pause.)

With the next breath, the attention moves up to the right thigh. The top of the thigh, from the knee up to the hip. Each breath fills the thigh with air, nearly weightless, like a balloon floating on the breeze. Now, the attention flows to the back of the thigh, along the hamstring, and up to the buttock with each new breath. (Pause.)

And now the attention moves back into the pelvis. The breath fills the pelvis. Experiencing the connection the back of the pelvis makes with the chair or the floor. The pelvic area relaxes as it fills with breath on every inhale, and releases with every exhale. (Pause.)

With the next breath, the awareness moves up the body, through the torso, to the shoulders, and then descends the left arm, and comes to rest on the left hand. Feeling the left hand cradled in the right or gently resting on the knee or by the side of the body. And as the next breath enters the body, the attention focuses on the left thumb. For this moment, there is only the left thumb and nothing else. Attending to the tip of your left thumb, the thumbnail, the knuckle. (Pause.) Now the attention moves to the forefinger … middle finger … ring finger … and finally, the little finger. The attention holds on just the fingers and thumb of the left hand for a moment. (Pause.)

Now the attention flows into the palm of the left hand. First the back of the left hand, the contact with the skin of the right, or the sensation of air flowing over it. The left hand becomes very light, filled with air, like a balloon. (Pause.)

And now, the awareness flows up into the left forearm, moving slowly from wrist to the elbow. Let the forearm fill with air. Sense the elbow and the tender flesh at the crook of the arm.

Allow the awareness to move into the bicep, filling with air like a balloon. Now sense the back of the upper arm from the elbow to the shoulder. Breathe. (Pause.)

The left shoulder becomes a balloon, inflating and becoming lighter with every inhalation.

And now the attention flows down the right arm until it settles in the right hand. As the next breath comes in, let the awareness focus in the right thumb. Sensing just the tip of the right thumb for a moment. (Pause.) Now move the attention to the forefinger … middle finger … ring finger … and finally, the little finger. Hold the attention just on the fingers and thumb of the right hand for a moment. (Pause.)

Now let the awareness flow into the palm of the right hand. Feel the slight weight of the left hand as it rests on the right palm, the contact with the skin. Let the right hand become very light, filled with air, like a balloon.

And now the awareness flows up into the right forearm, moving slowly from wrist to the elbow. The forearm fills with air with each breath. Sense the elbow and the flesh at the crook of the right arm.

Move the attention into the right bicep, filling it with air, releasing any tension. Now sense the back of the upper arm from the elbow to the shoulder. Breathe. (Pause.)

Let the right shoulder become a balloon, inflating and becoming lighter with every inhalation. (Pause.)

Now the attention floats up into the head. The head is a balloon, inflating a little more with each intake of breath. Floating on top of the shoulders, nearly weightless. (Pause.)

Imagine a string attached to the very top of the head, lightly pulling up toward the sky, lengthening the spine, raising the energy of the body toward the clouds. (Pause.) And just for a moment, let the head float. Breathing. Fully relaxed.

> (Pause.)
> And now, let the attention flow back into the body, sensing arms ... and hands ... legs ... and feet. Let the breath fill the entire body for just a moment. Everything light. Everything relaxed.
> And when you are ready, let the attention release from the body to include the room around you, the sounds of your surroundings, and the presence of your friends.
> Open your eyes if they have been closed. Blink and look around. Feel free to stretch and move a bit as you come back to the present moment and the here and now.

If this has been an early group learning session, some discussion time may be in order. The instructor can ask general questions about the students' experiences. Some participants may have fallen asleep. This is normal. A gentle suggestion to try and keep their eyes open and softly focused next time may be of some use. But the general tone of the discussion should be non-judgmental and supportive. There is essentially no wrong way to do an exercise of this nature. The only things the practitioners should be encouraged to avoid are bodily tensions and critical self-judgments.

If the meditators have already been through the exercise several times and have become comfortable with the experience, the class or cohort can simply adjourn or move onto the next exercise.

As mentioned above, this exercise has been presented as a guided script, however, once the practitioners have become comfortable with the meditation instructions and process, the traditional body scan can most easily, and perhaps best, be done as an *internally guided* exercise. By internalizing the guidance, attention can be more fully focused on the internal sensations of the activity itself, which tends to heighten the impact and deepen the effect. The script, of course, does not have to be followed verbatim, but is intended to act as a general guide for a meditation that focuses in some detail on a kinesthetic sense of the body.

References

Arnett, J.J. (2000). Emerging adulthood: A theory of development from the late teens through the twenties. *American Psychologist*, 55(5), 469–480. doi:10.1037/0003-066X.55.5.46doi:9

Center for Collegiate Mental Health (2015). *2015 annual report*. Retrieved from https://files.eric.ed.gov/fulltext/ED572760.pdf.

Center for Collegiate Mental Health (2016). *2016 annual report*. Retrieved from https://sites.psu.edu/ccmh/files/2017/01/2016-Annual-Report-FINAL_2016_01_09-1gc2hj6.pdf.

Chiesa, A., & Malinowski, P. (2011). Mindfulness-based approaches: Are they all the same? *Journal of Clinical Psychology*, 67(4), 404–424. doi:10.1002/jclp.20776

Dam, N.T.V., Vugt, M.K.V., Vago, D.R., Schmalzl, L., Saron, C.D., Olendzki, A., … Meyer, D.E. (2018). Mind the hype: A critical evaluation and prescriptive agenda for research on mindfulness and meditation. *Perspectives on Psychological Science*, *13*(1), 36–61. doi:10.1177/1745691617709589

The Editors of *Time* (2016). *TIME mindfulness: The new science of health and happiness*. New York: Time Magazine.

Everly, G.S., & Lating, J.M. (2002). *A clinical guide to the treatment of human stress response* (second edition). New York: Kluwer Academic/Plenum.

Gilpin, G. (2006). *The Maharishi effect: A personal journey through the movement that transformed American spirituality*. New York: J.P. Tarcher/Penguin.

Goldberg, P. (2010). *American Veda: From Emerson and the Beatles to yoga and meditation: How Indian spirituality changed the West* (first edition). New York: Harmony Books.

Goleman, D., & Davidson, R.J. (2017). *Altered traits: Science reveals how meditation changes your mind, brain, and body*. New York: Avery.

Heffernan, V. (2015). Muddied meaning of "mindfulness." *The New York Times Magazine*.

Kabat-Zinn, J. (2013). *Full catastrophe living: Using the wisdom of your body and mind to face stress, pain, and illness* (revised and updated edition). New York: Bantam Books.

Lippelt, D.P., Hommel, B., & Colzato, L.S. (2014). Focused attention, open monitoring and loving kindness meditation: Effects on attention, conflict monitoring, and creativity – a review. *Frontiers in Psychology*, *5*(1083), 1–5. doi:10.3389/fpsyg.2014.01083

Lutz, A., Slagter, H.A., Dunne, J.D., & Davidson, R.J. (2008). Attention regulation and monitoring in meditation. *Trends in Cognitive Sciences*, *12*(4), 163–169.

Misra, R., McKean, M., West, S., & Russo, T. (2000). Academic stress of college students: Comparison of student and faculty perceptions. *College Student Journal*, *34*(2), 236–245.

Mrazek, M.D., Franklin, M.S., Phillips, D.T., Baird, B., & Schooler, J.W. (2013). Mindfulness training improves working memory capacity and GRE performance while reducing mind wandering. *Psychological Science*, *241*(5), 776–781.

Page, K. (Writer and Director). (2006). Transpersonal conversations: Charles T. Tart, Ph.D. In Transpersonal Conversations. Transpersonal Media. DVD.

Ram, D., & Lama Foundation. (1971). *Be here now, remember*. San Cristobal and New York: Lama Foundation.

Rogers, H.B. (2018, April 1). Holly Rogers interview by K. Page.

Segal, Z.V., Williams, J.M.G., & Teasdale, J.D. (2013). *Mindfulness-based cognitive therapy for depression* (second edition). New York: Guilford Press.

Tart, C.T. (1969). *Altered states of consciousness: A book of readings*. New York: Wiley.

Valentine, E.R., & Sweet, P.L.G. (1999). Meditation and attention: A comparison of the effects of concentrative and mindfulness meditation on sustained attention. *Mental Health, Religion & Culture*, *2*(1), 59–70. doi:10.1080/13674679908406332

Wieczner, J. (2016). Meditating, for love and money. *Fortune*.

Yogananda, P. (2007). *Autobiography of a yogi*. Nevada City: Crystal Clarity Publishers.

2

ATTENTION AND DISTRACTION IN THE DIGITAL AGE

On June 29, 2007, the first iPhone was released, representing the birth of mobile digital technology and its ubiquitous insertion into our lifestyles and behavior patterns. Around the same time, in September 2006, a social media networking site called Facebook, that started on Harvard's campus and had grown in popularity with college students around the country, was launched to everyone with a valid email address along with an age requirement of being 13 or older. The public launch of Facebook, in a general sense, marks the beginning of the social media paradigm that continues to impact, if not characterize, how we communicate with each other today. It is my contention that these two techno-cultural events truly mark the emergence of the postmodern digital age, rather than the proliferation of microminiaturized computers some two decades previously (Baym, 2015).

With the postmodern digital age, along with its mobile digital computing and social media communication ecospheres, has come unanticipated side effects including relational intermediation, where face-to-face interpersonal interactions have been significantly displaced by interactions through social media platforms, and digital distraction, which causes shortened or fragmented attention spans and a limited ability to focus on linear discourse (Gazzaley & Rosen, 2016). The behavior most often identified as responsible for this proliferate relational disruption and digital distraction is called media multi-tasking. Below, I will share some research studies that have investigated media multi-tasking and its potentially deleterious effects.

In a 2009 research study run by scientists from Stanford's Department of Communication and Department of Psychology and Neurosciences, several effects of heavy media multi-tasking were identified. The study, *Cognitive Control in Media Multitaskers* (Ophira, Nassb, & Wagner, 2009), demonstrated that heavy media multi-taskers were "more susceptible to interference from irrelevant environmental stimuli and from irrelevant representations in memory" (2009, p. 15583). Heavy media multi-taskers also performed poorly on a task-switching exercise compared to a group of light media multi-taskers, likely because of a reduced ability to filter out mental interference and irrelevant stimuli. This finding was ironic, given the central role that task-switching plays in multi-tasking and the fact that media multi-taskers will often defend their behavior on the grounds that their ability to task-switch is improved or enhanced by the practice itself, a claim this data clearly refutes. The researchers determined that their "results suggest that heavy media multitaskers are distracted by the multiple streams of media they are consuming" (Ophira et al., 2009, p. 15585). They also concluded that people who multi-tasked significantly less were perhaps better at directing their attention and filtering out distractions, which are certainly important skills for the college-aged emerging adult.

In another study performed by psychologists at the Department of Psychology of Michigan State University, the researchers found that media multi-tasking could be related to depression and social phobia (as pointed out in the last chapter, two of the most often reported complaints by college students requesting counseling); it was also a good predictor of self-reported feelings of depression and social anxiety (Becker, Alzahabi, & Hopwood, 2013). The authors of the study emphasized that there has been a tremendous increase in media multi-tasking within Western cultures, and that while general media use, specifically among American youth, had grown by 20% in the last decade, multi-tasking behaviors by the same demographic had grown by nearly 120% during that period (2013, p. 132). These Michigan State psychologists concluded that media multi-tasking, as a subset of overall media use, created a unique risk for psychosocial dysfunction, including symptoms of depression and social anxiety disorders (2013, p. 134).

In a more recent study, building in part on the research cited above, Canadian researchers looked at the effects of multi-tasking on attentional focus and self-reporting of distraction and mental errors in everyday life situations outside of laboratory conditions.

> Our findings suggest that increased levels of media multitasking are accompanied by a self-perceived withdrawal of attention to and awareness of present real-world events and experiences, as well as increased incidences of attention-failure induced cognitive errors in engaging with real-world events and challenges.
>
> *(Ralph, Thomson, Cheyne, & Smilek, 2014, p. 667)*

We also found that increased levels of media multitasking were associated with the unintentional capture of attention by off-task thoughts, as well as with volitional shifts of attention between on-task and off-task thoughts. This increased tendency to mind wander may reflect the increased distractibility of HMMs [heavy media multitaskers] compared to LMMs [light media multitaskers].

(Ralph et al., 2014, p. 667)

On a more speculative note, these researchers posited as one potential lens for interpreting their findings that:

media multitasking might produce results opposite to those produced by practices such as mindfulness training, which teaches individuals to bring wandering attention back to a single task or thought (MacLean et al., 2010; M. D. Mrazek, Franklin, Phillips, Baird, & Schooler, 2013; M. D. Mrazek, Smallwood, & Schooler, 2012). Although mindfulness training might boost endogenous executive control of attention, media multitasking might unintentionally atrophy endogenous executive control mechanisms and even further potentiate exogenous mechanisms. This proposition is consistent with the claims of Cain and Mitroff (2011) and Ophir et al. (2009) who suggested that, compared to heavy media multitaskers, light users appear to have greater "top-down" control.

(Ralph et al., 2014, p. 667, emphasis added)

In yet another report, entitled *The Relationship Between Cell Phone Use, Academic Performance, Anxiety, and Satisfaction with Life in College Students* (Lepp, Barkley, & Karpinski, 2014), researchers from Kent State University concluded: "For the population studied [college students], high frequency cell phone users tended to have lower GPA, higher anxiety, and lower satisfaction with life relative to their peers who used the cell phone less often" (2014, p. 348).

Not all research cited above has been fully replicated, as evidenced by a study, *Working Memory, Fluid Intelligence, and Impulsiveness in Heavy Media Multitaskers* (Minear, Brasher, McCurdy, Lewis, & Younggren, 2013), that failed to replicate Ophira et al.'s original findings regarding the task-switching deficits of heavy media multi-taskers; however, efforts to understand the impact of digital media, particularly multi-tasking behavior, continues.

From a slightly different perspective, researchers in Taiwan studied employees at 13 different business firms to assess the impact of social media addiction on mindfulness (which they defined essentially as focusing complete attention, without judgment, on the experiences of present moment reality), and emotional coping strategies and exhaustion (Sriwilai & Charoensukmongkol, 2015, p. 428). The findings of Sriwilai and Charoensukmongkol revealed that:

people who are highly addicted to social media tended to have lower mindfulness and tended to use emotion-focused coping to deal with stress. Lack of mindfulness and the decision to use emotion-coping strategy are also subsequently associated with higher emotional exhaustion.

(2015, p. 427)

Some of the most interesting work has involved looking at mindfulness practices as a potential antidote to the conditions of distraction that many students and adults find themselves in today. In this study published by *Scientific Reports*, researchers from the Department of Psychology at the University of Wisconsin-Madison explored using a short-term mindfulness training as a way to counteract the negative effects of heavy media multi-tasking. Their conclusions were:

> (1) that heavy media multitaskers showed generally poorer attentional abilities than light media multitaskers, and (2) that all participants showed benefits from the short-term mindfulness intervention. Furthermore, we found that the benefits of the short-term mindfulness intervention were not equivalently large across participants. Instead, these *benefits were disproportionately large in the heavy media multitaskers*. While the positive outcomes were short-lived, this opens the possibility of performing long-term interventions with the goal of realizing lasting gains in this population.
> (Gorman & Green, 2016, p. 1, emphasis added)

Another group of researchers tested female human resource workers from the San Francisco, California, and Seattle, Washington, areas to explore the effects of an eight-week meditation training on multi-tasking behavior in a high-stress work environment. They organized their participants into three groups for this study: one group did the meditation, one group was wait-listed and then did the meditation training, and the last group learned an unrelated type of body relaxation. The meditators, after training, were able to stay on task longer and switched tasks less often. The meditators also self-reported fewer negative emotions associated with the work they were asked to perform. Interestingly, both the meditation group and the relaxation group had demonstrably better memory recall of the tasks they performed during the testing (Levy, Wobbrock, Kaszniak, & Ostergren, 2012, p. 45).

In their popular treatise, *The Distracted Mind* (2016), researchers Adam Gazzaley and Larry D. Rosen, a neuroscientist and a psychologist respectively, review an enormous amount of data, including most of the studies cited above, to create an accessible model of consciousness-based goal setting and evaluate the effects the technology wave appears to be having on first-world populations to function at full proficiency. In their view:

> Complex, interwoven, time-delayed, and often shared goals are what allow us humans to exert an unprecedented influence over how we interact with the world around us, navigating its multifaceted environments based on our decisions rather than reflexive responses to our surroundings [animal-like instincts] …
>
> Our proficiency in setting goals is mediated by a collection of cognitive abilities that are widely known as "executive functions," a set of skills that include evaluation, decision making, organization, and planning … Our

> ability to effectively carry out our goals is dependent on an assemblage of related cognitive abilities that we will refer to ... as "cognitive control." This includes attention, working memory, and goal management ... Our cognitive control abilities that are necessary for the enactment of our goals have not evolved to the same degree as the executive functions required for goal setting ... [W]e have a restricted ability to distribute, divide, and sustain attention; actively hold detailed information in mind; and concurrently manage or even rapidly switch between competing goals.
>
> *(Gazzaley & Rosen, 2016, pp. 8–9)*

They go on to propose that humans, in a biological, evolutionary sense, are *information foragers* in a similar way to our history as food foragers; that it is fundamental to our survival that we forage effectively for information within our environment; and that millions of years of evolution has selected for this trait. They then make a convincing argument that the latest wave of information technology, which includes the Internet, social networks, and mobile-digital technology, is both a natural outgrowth of our information foraging behavior *and* that the technologies themselves have outstripped our abilities to efficiently use our cognitive control abilities, the most important of which, according to the authors, is the attention function (Gazzaley & Rosen, 2016, pp. 29–34). Interestingly, toward the end of the book, where the authors offer practices and solutions to the mounting problems coming from the conflict between technology's demands and our neurological processing limitations, they point to meditation practice as one of the most promising solutions currently available (Gazzaley & Rosen, 2016, pp. 188–190).

While this review of the research on distraction and media multi-tasking is far from exhaustive, it does support the idea that the current populations of students on university campuses are more likely to have fragmented attention spans and varying degrees of digital distraction than students of the past. In light of these findings, I think we need to ask how our universities are directly addressing the attention function of our students. Are they taking this cultural shift toward multiple information streams seriously enough? What sorts of remedies or interventions are being built into the college curriculum? If the attention spans and emotional lives of the students that are coming into our universities today have been fundamentally altered, do we not have a compelling need to look at how our pedagogies can help, rather than ignore, this newly emergent reality?

One approach to this problem, although not a panacea or comprehensive solution, is the introduction of mindfulness-based training as suggested by several of the studies noted above. In many university systems now, formal and informal mindfulness-based training is being offered through university health and counseling programs, student-led organizations, and individual professors that have developed their own training protocols appropriate to their individual institution or resource sets.

In their 2008 research review, *Toward the Integration of Meditation into Higher Education* (Shapiro, Brown, & Astin, 2008), researchers identified three primary areas that mindfulness training (meaning both the practice of meditation and the cultivated state of mindfulness as a result of practice) could make significant impacts on the post-secondary educational environment. These areas included improved cognitive and academic performance; decreased states of stress, anxiety, and depression as well as better regulation of emotional reactions; and the development of the "whole person," which included areas such as creativity and improved interpersonal relationships. In particular, they noted the importance of the attention function to learning and the increasing fragmentation of attention in our postmodern society. They then went on to conclude:

> Despite its importance to learning, focused attention is rarely if ever systematically trained or cultivated in most educational settings. And yet, attentional training has been the hallmark of meditative disciplines for centuries, and thus the incorporation of these practices into higher education could be of great benefit.
> *(Shapiro et al., 2008, p. 10)*

So, how can we directly train the attention function using meditation practices in the university setting? We have already looked at the body scan as a type of concentration meditation that focuses on individual body parts in a systematic order. Below, we will introduce a traditional type of FAM that emphasizes attention to a single point of focus: the breath-cycle.

Focused Attention Meditation (FAM) on the Breath

Perhaps the most common object of attention in FAM is the breath. Breathing is a ubiquitous activity that everyone does. Breath is essential to life; and its rhythms, whether we're conscious of them or not, follow us through all our days and even into sleep. Breathing is a primary physical function that is self-regulating and constant. You can always find the sensation of your own breathing, no matter where you are, and therefore breath really is an ideal object of attention for a meditation exercise.

Below, I will once again present a scripted/guided version of the basic instructions and process for *FAM on the Breath*. However, you can certainly learn these instructions through practice in the first couple of weeks of training and then internalize the activity so that you eventually can sit very still and quietly, with your breath as your *only* focus during your session.

The initial instructions are almost identical to those in the *Traditional Body Scan* exercise, but I will reproduce them below for the convenience of the narrator or guide.

FAM ON THE BREATH

Instructions:

No cellphones or digital devices should be present in the room during this exercise, even vibration alerts are distracting. So, power the devices completely off and put them away, out of sight, before the session begins.

Sit on the floor on a cushion or mat and a meditation pillow to elevate your buttocks slightly above your knees (if you are sitting cross-legged). You can also sit on a chair with your feet on the ground in front of you, shoulder-width apart. Place your hands, palms up in your lap, right hand cradling left, with thumb tips lightly touching. Your hands and arms should be relaxed. You can also place your hands palms down on your thighs. Once you've found your position, settle in and allow your awareness to turn inward.

You can also lie on the floor for this exercise. You may want to use a yoga mat and some low pillows to support your neck and slightly raise the knees. Place your hands comfortably at your sides, either palms up or down. Hands can also be draped lightly on top of your abdomen but avoid interlocking the fingers. The goal is to remain comfortably in this position for up to half an hour without the need to overly shift or adjust your position. Relaxation will be an integral part of this exercise.

This exercise can also be done in a standing position. Center yourself over your feet which should be shoulder-width apart. Your feet remain relaxed but firmly planted, knees unlocked and slightly bent, pelvis tucked slightly under your torso, spine erect and arms loose at your sides with palms turned naturally in toward the thighs, your elbows slightly bent, hands relaxed and fingers slightly curled. You may want to gently roll your shoulders a couple of times, allowing the chest to open as you settle into a relaxed, aligned position. Again, the goal is to remain comfortably in this position for up to half an hour without the need to overly shift or adjust your position.

While you can close your eyes, I recommend keeping them open and softly focused. If you are seated, you can let your eyelids droop slightly and pick a spot on the floor between three and five feet in front of you, where you can focus without straining. Again, you want a soft focus so that while individual objects may be slightly blurred, you are still able to see the objects in your immediate field of vision. If you are lying down, pick an area of the ceiling (or sky) that you can gaze upon easily, again, without staring. The point is to *stay awake and alert* for the duration of the exercise without falling asleep or causing tension in the eyes. If you choose to close your eyes, be warned that this often can lead to sleep, which is not our goal; and so, if you find yourself drifting out of consciousness, you may want to open your eyes, blink a few times, and maintain a soft focus as you continue.

Unless you otherwise cannot, due to blocked airways or the like, it is recommended that you keep your mouth closed during all meditation exercises and *breath through your nose.* While your mouth is closed, allow your tongue to rest, pressed gently against the front teeth. This will prevent excessive salivation and swallowing, which can be a distraction during an extended session.

Guidance Script:

Take a moment to settle into the body. Release any tensions and allow the awareness to focus on breathing.

Simply experience the body breathing for the next five breaths. (Pause.)

As the breath enters and leaves the body in its natural rhythm, continue to release any tensions that come into awareness. As each breath enters the body, notice the sensation of coolness at the tip of the nostrils where the air enters. Experience that sensation of coolness completely.

As each breath enters the body, it makes a journey from the nose down through the chest, where it expands the belly as it fills the body with life-giving air. Follow the path of the breath as it makes its journey ... first in at the nostrils, then expanding the belly, then filling the chest. There is a pause ... and then notice the chest begin to fall and the belly contract as the exhalation cycle begins. (Pause.)

Follow this entire process, being fully aware of each sensation, for the next few breath cycles. (Pause.)

With each breath cycle, let go of a little more tension, allowing relaxation to deepen, the body becoming full of air, light as a balloon drifting on a cloud. (Pause.)

And if the mind wanders, as it inevitably will, simply acknowledge whatever has captured the attention in a non-judgmental way, identifying the thought, emotion, or memory and letting it go, gently but firmly returning attention once more to the breath. [Repeat as necessary.] (Pause.)

Imagine a string coming out of the top of the head, a balloon attached at the end, gently pulling the top of the head upwards, floating, spine straight, lengthening, relaxed ... continuing to breathe. (Pause.)

Simply become aware of the sensation of breathing in ... and breathing out ... breathing in ... and breathing out. [Repeat as necessary.] (Pause.)

Be aware of this breath ... and this breath ... and this breath. Each breath is unique: savor it. [Repeat as necessary.] (Pause.)

Be with the breath ... relax into the breath ... let the breath help the body to float ... this breath ... and this breath ... and this breath. [Repeat as necessary.] (Pause.)

When thoughts enter the mind, notice the thought, imagine the thought as a cloud ... and let it float away as you return to the very next in-breath. [Repeat as necessary.] (Pause.)

Slowly and gently, when you are ready, allow your awareness to expand to include the room around you, the activity in the space, and the presence of your friends.

As before, with the *Traditional Body Scan*, depending on the speed with which the narrator/leader reads through the script, the number of repetitions of the various sections, and the lengths of the experiential pauses allowed, a *FAM on the Breath* meditation session can last anywhere from ten minutes to a full hour. The script does not have to be followed verbatim but is intended to act as a general guide for a meditation that focuses on a kinesthetic sense of the breathing process.

Counting or Labeling Breaths

Once you have mastered and internalized the instructions and technique presented above in guided form, you may do this meditation regularly without guidance. One useful tool that many practitioners use, particularly in the first months when they are simply learning to maintain a state of relaxed-but-aware concentration, is *counting the breathes* or *labeling the breaths*. This is how it works. Once you settle into your meditative posture and turn your attention to an awareness of your breath, silently count "one" on the inhale, staying aware of the sensation of inhalation all the way through until the pause that occurs before exhalation. As the exhalation cycle begins, once again count silently, "two," staying with the exhalation sensation until it is complete. With the next inhalation, count "three" and so forth until reaching the number ten. Then begin the sequence over again with the number "one" on the next inhale. All the counting is internal and done *silently*; avoid mouthing, whispering, or mumbling the numbers. This counting process can be very useful in helping focus fully on the sensation of your inhalation and exhalation cycle, particularly in the early stages when you are learning to stabilize your attention function.

When you discover that your mind has wandered (as you inevitably will), gently release whatever thought, memory, or emotion that has captured your attention and begin again with the number "one" on the next inhalation that you take. Eventually, you will drop the counting of breathes altogether and simply follow the course of your own breathing in real-time; but for now, try counting breaths once you "graduate" from the guided version of the exercise.

As an alternative to the counting of the breathes, you can simply "label" the breathing process by thinking silently to yourself on the inhalation cycle, "inhale," and then "exhale" when the breath begins to leave your body. In either case, counting or labeling, the intention is to keep the attention gently but firmly focused on the process of breathing, *not* the counting or labeling. So be forewarned to avoid letting the act of counting or labeling become the focus of the exercise. This activity is not meant as a chant or some rhythmic object of attention, but as a device to help you constantly re-direct your attention to the simple and natural sensation of breathing. Chanting or "phrase repetition," as an object of meditation, is a somewhat different process and will be discussed in some detail in a later chapter.

References

Baym, N.K. (2015). *Personal connections in the digital age* (second edition). Malden, MA: Polity Press.

Becker, M.W., Alzahabi, R., & Hopwood, C.J. (2013). Media multitasking is associated with symptoms of depression and social anxiety. *Cyberpsychology, Behavior, and Social Networking, 16*(2), 132–135.

Gazzaley, A., & Rosen, L.D. (2016). *The distracted mind: Ancient brains in a high-tech world.* Cambridge, MA: MIT Press.

Gorman, T.E., & Green, C.S. (2016). Short-term mindfulness intervention reduces the negative attentional effects associated with heavy media multitasking. *Scientific Reports, 6,* 24542.

Lepp, A., Barkley, J.E., & Karpinski, A.C. (2014). The relationship between cell phone use, academic performance, anxiety, and satisfaction with life in college students. *Computers in Human Behavior, 31,* 343–350.

Levy, D.M., Wobbrock, J.O., Kaszniak, A.W., & Ostergren, M. (2012). The effects of mindfulness meditation training on multitasking in a high-stress information environment. Paper presented at the Proceedings of Graphics Interface 2012, Toronto, Ontario, Canada.

Minear, M., Brasher, F., McCurdy, M., Lewis, J., & Younggren, A. (2013). Working memory, fluid intelligence, and impulsiveness in heavy media multitaskers. *Psychonomic Bulletin & Review, 20*(6), 1274–1281.

Ophira, E., Nassb, C., & Wagner, A.D. (2009). Cognitive control in media multitaskers. *Proceedings of the National Academy of Sciences, 106*(37), 15583–15587.

Ralph, B.C.W., Thomson, D.R., Cheyne, J.A., & Smilek, D. (2014). Media multitasking and failures of attention in everyday life. *Psychological Research, 78*(5), 661–669.

Shapiro, S., Brown, K.W, & Astin, J. (2011). Toward the integration of meditation into higher education: A review of research evidence. *Teachers College Record, 113*(3), 493–528.

Sriwilai, K., & Charoensukmongkol, P. (2015). Face it, don't Facebook it: Impacts of social media addiction on mindfulness, coping strategies and the consequence on emotional exhaustion. *Stress and Health, 32,* 427–434.

3

WHAT IS MBSR (AND WHAT IT IS NOT)?

Jon Kabat-Zinn is a master meditation teacher with a degree in molecular biology. As briefly mentioned in Chapter 1, in 1979 he began hosting a clinic to teach secularized meditation practices to medical patients who were experiencing chronic pain and stress-related disorders. He called his program Mindfulness-Based Stress Reduction (MBSR) and it has now proliferated throughout the Western medical community taught by over 1,000 certified instructors in more than 700 medical settings in over 30 countries (Kabat-Zinn, 2013, p. xlvii). Kabat-Zinn's own program, at the University of Massachusetts Medical Center Hospital, has trained more than 24,000 people in MBSR practices, and spawned a wave of research into mindfulness (as both a meditation style and a state of consciousness). But what actually is MBSR and how does it function in the medical setting?

MBSR today is a clinically delivered, eight-week program, in the branch of medicine now known as mind/body or integrative medicine. It is an intervention intended to act upon the self-awareness and basic consciousness of patients suffering from a wide variety of physical illness and stress-induced conditions ranging from headaches, high blood pressure, back pain, heart disease, cancer, AIDS, PTSD, depression, and anxiety. The MBSR program is administered as a *complement* to traditional medical treatment (not a replacement for it), the general theory being that our thinking and behavior can have significant impacts on physical health and the ability to recover from illness, and MBSR has been shown to have positive effects on thinking patterns, psychological well-being, and quality of life (Kabat-Zinn, 2013; Will et al., 2015).

When first introduced, in 1979, by Kabat-Zinn at the UMass Medical Center Hospital, the concept of meditation training was considered radical and speculative. As mentioned in Chapter 1, in 1969 there were only three articles available in Western medical or psychological peer-reviewed journals on meditation practice (Tart, 1969). Kabat-Zinn himself first started a personal meditation practice in 1966 while a graduate student at MIT (Kabat-Zinn, 2011). In his early professional career, Kabat-Zinn was a faculty member in the Biology Department at Brandeis University teaching molecular genetics and a science class for non-science majors. He also spent time as director of the Cambridge Zen Center and taught large mindful yoga classes weekly in a church in Harvard Square. In addition, he would occasionally offer meditation training and yoga/stretching workshops for athletes, especially runners (Kabat-Zinn, 2011). In 1976, he joined the University of Massachusetts Medical School as a research associate and later, postdoctoral fellow in the Anatomy and Cell Biology Department. This appointment would turn out to be fortuitous for the young molecular biologist not only professionally but as a way that would ultimately lead to his personal goal of introducing mindfulness training into Western medicine.

During a two-week meditation retreat in 1979, Kabat-Zinn had what he has described as a very short "vision" in which he conceptualized a way to deliver the types of meditation training he had been learning and teaching for more than a dozen years at that point to the general public; people who, in his estimation, would not normally or willing go to a meditation or yoga center to get it. In telling this story, Kabat-Zinn points out that at that point in history, meditation and yoga centers were still very rare in America and considered exotic organizations that very few Westerners yet understood or would intentionally engage with, severely limiting the average citizen's access to the practices that Kabat-Zinn saw as potentially healing and transformative. "I saw in a flash not only a model that could be put in place, but also the long-term implications of what might happen if the basic idea was sound" (Kabat-Zinn, 2011).

His idea was essentially simple. Create a program in everyday language that typical Americans could understand and accept, that would present the basics of a primarily Buddhist meditation practice in a common-sense secular framework without the esoteric language and complex philosophical trappings that historically had been common practice for transmitting these traditions. While he did not have the language for it at the time, Kabat-Zinn's primary realization was that, in order to reach large segments of American secular culture, he would need to strip the traditional practices of their religious and cultural trappings in order to deliver the essence, and what he clearly identified as the benefits, of the practices in a way that could be broadly accepted. It then quickly occurred to him that the hospital that he was currently working in might be the perfect test ground for such a program.

> What better place than a hospital to make the dharma available to people in ways that they might possibly understand it and be inspired by a heartfelt and practical invitation to explore whether it might not be possible to do something *for themselves* as a complement to their more traditional medical treatments.
>
> *(Kabat-Zinn, 2011, p. 297, emphasis in original)*

His approach was to reframe the training protocol for basic mindfulness meditation practice and simple yoga exercises and describe them operationally, in terms of the self-regulation of attention.

> The intention and approach behind MBSR were never meant to exploit, fragment, or decontextualize the dharma [traditional spiritual context of Buddhist meditation practice], but rather to recontextualize it within the frameworks of science, medicine (including psychiatry and psychology), and health care so that it would be maximally useful to people who could not hear it or enter into it through the more traditional [ways] … whether they were doctors or medical patients, hospital administrators, or insurance companies.
>
> *(Kabat-Zinn, 2011, p. 298)*

Given there was already a growing literature related to the psychophysiology of stress reactivity and pain regulation, Kabat-Zinn decided to name his approach "stress reduction" (instead of using the word meditation). However, by the early 1990s, he felt like he needed to expand the term to help distinguish his program from others that included the term stress reduction or stress management, and so added the descriptor "mindfulness-based," and so the acronym most popularly used today, MBSR, was born.

Kabat-Zinn acknowledges the numerous traditional influences on the process that ultimately became the standardized MBSR training protocol, including (at a minimum): Theravada (Kornfield, 1977; Nyanaponika, 1969) and Mahayana Buddhist roots within both the Soto (Suzuki & Dixon, 1970) and Rinzai (Kapleau, 1966) Zen traditions (and by lineage, the earlier Chinese and Korean streams), as well as certain currents from the yogic traditions, including Vedanta (Nisargadatta, 1973), the teachings of J. Krishnamurti (Krishnamurti, 1969, 1979) and Ramana Maharshi (Ramana & Osborne, 1959). Some of the other influences that he acknowledges, include: *Meditation in Action* (Trungpa, 1969), *The Miracle of Mindfulness* (Nhất, 1976), and *The Experience of Insight* (Goldstein, 1976). He also gathered much of the Western research available at that time to help clarify and justify his thinking from an empirical perspective. This included early papers by Daniel Goleman and Richard Davidson (Davidson, Goleman, & Schwartz, 1976; Goleman & Schwartz, 1976); the work of Herbert Benson on the relaxation response (Benson, 1975); and the work of Roger Walsh, including his seminal 1980 paper, "The Consciousness Disciplines and the Behavioral Sciences: Questions of Comparison and Assessment," published in the *American Journal of Psychiatry* (Walsh, 1977, 1978, 1980).

In 1990, Kabat-Zinn published the seminal *Full Catastrophe Living: Using the Wisdom of Your Body and Mind to Face Stress, Pain, and Illness*. In this book, he lays out in simple terms the precepts and protocol of his MBSR program. He also produced a number of audio tapes containing the guided instructions for the various meditation and yoga exercises used in the standard MBSR program.

The program Kabat-Zinn started in 1979 has now grown into The Center for Mindfulness in Medicine, Health Care, and Society, and is officially categorized as the Division of Mindfulness within the Department of Medicine at the University of Massachusetts Medical School. The Center for Mindfulness includes the stress reduction clinic where MBSR training is still offered to patients of the hospital and the general public, as well as the Oasis Institute which provides professional training and MBSR teacher certification programs.

The basic protocols for the delivery of the eight-week MBSR training are generally standardized, although continually updated, and all certified teachers of the program are expected to maintain a rigorous personal practice of meditation that includes regular silent retreats. The certification process is required to offer MBSR training to the public with the designation of Center for Mindfulness (CFM) Certified MBSR Teacher and takes approximately a year to complete. The teacher training includes a number of on-site trainings, individual mentoring and supervision, and mandatory silent retreats. While the curriculum is codified, each MBSR teacher will still bring a unique individual perspective to imparting the training and there is some variation in what is allowed in the MBSR sequence. Following is a general outline of the MBSR course and its content.

The MBSR Eight-Week Course

MBSR is conceived of as a group intervention. As such, it has some basic built-in differences from the traditional student–guru delivery structure of the meditation systems that it is based on. While open communication and questioning of the group leader is encouraged, one of the more important ingredients of the eight-week program is *group process*. MBSR teachers are specifically trained to encourage and cultivate this group process during their classes so that the students, to the greatest extent possible, make discoveries and answer questions *for themselves* through direct experience. Also, as many of the participants will inevitably be dealing with issues of pain, illness, or psychological distress (often the reasons they enter the program in the first place), each participant is pre-screened by the instructor to identify any contra-indicated conditions, which can include (but are not limited to), active substance abuse/dependence, suicidal ideation, symptoms of untreated psychosis, PTSD, major depression, extreme social anxiety, etc. While certain of these preconditions can actually be treated with other types of mindfulness-based interventions, they may require more of a clinical setting or a therapist/client relationship to be effective and mostly preclude safely participating in the open group process structure, making the MBSR class an inappropriate choice for certain people. The pre-screening can be delivered in a number of forms, from an Internet intake form, to a pre-session meeting or individual interview. The screened participants are asked to sign an informed consent and waiver form either before or during the first class.

The first weekly session usually includes some form of round-robin introductions and an explication of the rules for group participation and expectations for individual conduct and commitment. These rules and expectations include: an agreement of confidentiality among participants, a firm commitment to attend all classes (including a full-day retreat later in the sequence) and to do all outside-of-class exercises (which includes at least 45 minutes a day of meditation work throughout the duration of the course), and an acceptance of the responsibility to participate in the group process.

The weekly meetings follow a predetermined sequence that generally involve two or more meditation or mindful yoga exercises, a group discussion on topics such as emotional reactivity, the experience of mindfulness in daily life, emotional attachments, relationships, positive and negative life experiences, difficult encounters, and stress and stressors. In addition to gentle but active yoga exercises, each style of meditation practice is introduced in turn, starting with a body scan meditation, then moving to a seated breathing practice, a walking meditation, and finally an open-monitoring style (often called "choiceless awareness") that cycles through an attentional shifting through all of the senses and finally all of experience as it arises in the moment, which includes mental events such as thoughts/feelings/emotions/memories, etc. Participants are expected to perform various meditation and yoga practices on a daily basis between class sessions. This "homework" is essential in establishing the experiential dimension of the learning and participants are often assigned to keep a journal record of their personal practice time both to encourage participation and to act as a lens for evaluating progress. Home practice also includes informal mindfulness exercises such as mindful eating, mindful bathing, or other activities (often habitual) that can be used to cultivate a general mindful attitude.

Between the sixth class and the seventh class, all participants are expected to attend a full-day silent retreat experience, led by the instructor, that typically lasts for six hours. Retreat activities include all of the meditation and yoga forms the students have learned to date, all performed in total vocal silence, plus the lunchtime meal is consumed in silence as an informal mindful eating practice.

The focus of MBSR as a medical intervention informs the delivery, content, and target demographic for the program. Primarily aimed at an adult population suffering from chronic pain or stress related illness, the MBSR program is not necessarily the most appropriate for an otherwise healthy college-aged population which will have its own primary concerns and goals that may be very different from an adult medical patient population. College-aged populations, often called emerging adults (Arnett, 2000), may indeed be having issues with stress, as discussed in Chapter 1, however, they also tend to have their own emotional/developmental concerns such as role identity, intimate relationships, and anxiety over their future place in the world. To more specifically speak to an emerging-adult population of college-aged students, Dr. Holly Rogers and Dr. Margaret Maytan of Duke University developed a program they ultimately named Koru that is specifically targeted for an emerging-adult population and their unique need-set and concerns (Rogers, 2016; Rogers & Maytan, 2012).

Koru Training for Emerging Adults

In 1996, Dr. Holly Rogers began working in the Duke University Student Counseling Center. A long-time meditator herself, Rogers quickly identified that many of her student clients were suffering from stress-related complaints that might be helped by meditation practice. However, after numerous attempts to train students in traditional types of meditation practice, Rogers found that it was very difficult to get her student clients to take up the practice in a meaningful way that would help them with their specific types of collegiate-oriented stress problems. After multiple attempts to structure a class in meditative techniques for college students, she began collaborating with a colleague, Margaret Maytan, who had been through a training program provided by the Center for Mind-Body Medicine (CMBM) (Rogers, 2018). CMBM's approach to wellness utilized practical, evidence-based skills for self-care, nutrition, self-awareness, and group support, including mind-body techniques such as meditation, biofeedback, guided imagery, and self-expression (The Center for Mind-Body Medicine, 2018). Together, they began a trial-and-error process of developing a delivery system for meditation and other self-care practices that would be customized to a college student population and make a more significant impact than both of their earlier efforts had yielded.

Eventually, the pair hit on a four-week structure that consisted of one 75-minute class session per week and a set of very short homework exercises for non-class days that they entitled "Koru". Koru is a word borrowed from the Māori people of New Zealand (an Eastern Polynesian indigenous population to the area) that refers to the spiral shape of an unfurling fern frond. The term is intended to symbolize newly developing life, balance, and harmony, all characteristics that the Koru program endeavors to foster in its college student demographic. Much like the MBSR program discussed above, Koru features small-group interactions over didactic instruction in order to keep the process experiential. While a Koru group is not a traditional group process or therapy encounter (students are not encouraged to discuss their personal problems and conflicts per se), the student participants are encouraged to share the challenges and rewards they experience with their out-of-class skills practice. The teaching of mindfulness practices as well as stress-coping skills is primarily transmitted through this type of group interaction, which in the class structure is called "checking in." By using this checking-in technique, the instructors are able to utilize the struggles and individual examples supplied by the students' experience to illuminate and clarify the essential features of the exercises they are teaching (Rogers & Maytan, 2012, p. 9).

While there are many similarities between Koru and MBSR training, there are also significant differences. Interestingly, while Rogers acknowledges the general influence that MBSR has had on the field of mindfulness as a whole, neither her nor Maytan had ever completed MBSR training and developed their own protocol specifically with emerging-adult college students in mind, rather than the population of adult pain and stress patients that MBSR is mainly intended to address (Rogers, 2018). Specifically, the context of the group discussions and organization of content delivery is centered around subject matters more germane to a college audience such as concern over identity and future roles, controlling anxiety in new situations, responsibilities often confronted for the first time by emerging adults, and relationship struggles. Another example is that the meditation sessions prescribed both during class sessions and as homework are only ten minutes in length, as opposed to 45 minutes to an hour with traditional MBSR. By utilizing their unique format of checking-in and the topic focus curated for the target age demographic, the architects of Koru have created a program that has far more relevance to college-aged students than the more medically oriented (and challenging) MBSR program.

The initial four-week sequence, which Rogers considers their "basic" course, has been captured for potential teachers of Koru in the 2012 book, *Mindfulness for the Next Generation: Helping Emerging Adults Manage Stress and Lead Healthier Lives* (Rogers & Maytan, 2012), with a follow-up volume authored by Rogers alone, entitled *The Mindful Twenty-Something: Life Skills to Handle Stress & Everything Else* (2016), addressed directly to the students of Koru.

In 2014, Rogers started the Center for Koru Mindfulness and began certification training specifically on the Koru model. The Center has trained and certified over 360 Koru teachers as of this writing (Rogers, 2018). As with MBSR, Koru-certified teachers are required and encouraged to maintain a personal mindfulness practice.

The Koru Four-Week Sequence

As mentioned above, the basic Koru program is a four-week sequence originally offered through the Student Counseling Center on a non-credit basis. The sequence is now offered at various centers around the Duke campus and in the dorms. The class size is limited to 12–15 student participants and the ten-minute-a-day homework assignments are mandatory. Attendance at all four class sessions is mandatory for successful completion of the sequence. The students are also required to keep a daily log of their out-of-class practice sessions which are reviewed but not graded by the course instructor. The four-week structure and the very brief length of homework assignments proved to be the most successful in the Duke University environment and Rogers holds that this formula has allowed Koru to reach the broadest possible number of students in her given environment (Rogers, 2018).

The mandatory nature of class attendance and completion of homework assignments is an important ingredient of the experiential learning model Koru is based upon. As Koru is primarily delivered to active college students enrolled in a formal university environment, the students tend to be familiar with mandatory requirements and comply more readily with this structure than independent adults might be inclined to do. The value and effects of meditation training are almost wholly derived from the actual repetition, on a regular basis over time, of the experiential exercises and so requiring the students to do the experiential work is fundamental to the success of the Koru program.

The first class session begins with a short guided breathing meditation and a "check-in" which primarily consists of participant introductions and an articulation of why the students have elected to attend and their personal goals for the class. The vast majority tend to identify stress and stress management as the primary reason for an interest in Koru (Rogers, 2018). Given this reality of emerging-adult college student life, the first class session is explicitly designed to give the participants immediately accessible tools for dealing with stress in daily life. These exercises include a basic version of diaphragmatic breathing ("belly breathing"), dynamic breathing (in Koru this is labeled "chicken breath" as an amusing analogy between the rapid up-and-down movement of the arms and the flapping of a chicken's wings), and a body scan meditation sequence similar to (but generally of shorter duration than) the body scan presented in MBSR training (Rogers & Maytan, 2012, pp. 69–81).

The second class session begins with a short breathing meditation and the check-in process. Usually the check-in process in the second week takes more time than the first because the students have had a week of experience they want to discuss and often have many questions. This is where the group process dynamic is very helpful in both engaging the students' curiosity and in transmitting additional instruction. The instructors will discuss the meditation logs that were submitted over the preceding week through the Koru app. The new exercise introduced in week two is a walking meditation which provides a nice alternative to the more sedentary seated and lying down practices introduced in week one. This session also introduces "gathas" (or meditation poems) as a way to deepen the focus of attention on the breath during seated meditation (Rogers & Maytan, 2012, pp. 83–95).

In the third week, a guided imagery exercise is introduced as a way to deal with stress and cultivate relaxation. The students are also led through a meditation where they learn to label (and let go of) thoughts and thought processes. Random thoughts and obsessive thinking patterns are often a major obstacle to the students during the course of Koru training and learning to deal more effectively with distracting thoughts can be a very useful self-moderating skill (Rogers & Maytan, 2012, pp. 97–110).

Much of the fourth and final Koru class is centered around encouraging and empowering students to continue their practice beyond the formal Koru class training. Opening meditation is taken, and the check-in process is engaged. In this class, students are introduced to the concept of mindful eating, and extending the context of mindfulness into other habitual areas of their lives (what we call in CMT "informal mindfulness practice," discussed more fully in Chapter 4). The final skill to be introduced is a meditation where the labeling of feelings is the focus (much like the labeling of thoughts was in the previous class) (Rogers & Maytan, 2012, pp. 111–121).

In Rogers and Maytan's program, an additional sequence of four weeks is made available under the title Koru 2.0 that includes longer daily homework sessions (usually 20 minutes a day), as well as additional training in loving kindness and a seated yoga series (Rogers, 2018).

During 2012–2013, Rogers and others ran a randomized controlled trial of the Koru program at Duke University, assessing the results of 90 participants against a wait-listed control group. This initial trial showed significant changes in perceived stress, sleep problems, mindfulness, and self-compassion (Greeson, Juberg, Maytan, James, & Rogers, 2014).

To support the Koru program and its proliferation throughout college-aged student populations, Rogers has developed an app that acts both as a meditation timer and digital log so that teachers and students can interact more directly with each other in establishing and documenting the out-of-class practice. The Koru app's design includes a teacher's dashboard that aggregates student practice data in one place and makes it easier for teachers to respond individually with comments and encouragement over a digital platform instead of the handwritten physical log books (Rogers, 2018).

College Mindfulness Training (CMT)

College Mindfulness Training (CMT) consists of a specific protocol of activities that have been influenced by, but are unique from (in organization, sequence, and dosage), MBSR training, Koru mindfulness, traditional meditation training, and a program designed for conservatory acting students as presented in *Advanced Consciousness Training (A.C.T.) for Actors* (Page, 2018). While MBSR is delivered over an eight-week sequence to adults with medical, pain, and stress-related illness, and Koru is a four-week non-credit-bearing course for college-aged students, CMT has been designed as a full semester credit-bearing course of instruction both on the academic and experiential levels. The CMT protocol can also be utilized by individuals interested in self-training with a minimum of adaptation (see Chapters 8 and 9 for programmatic recommendations).

CMT, as presented in this book, includes a full menu of experiential exercises that will give students a basic program of practice composed of both FAM and OMM that, when taken together, can become the basis of a life-long developmental practice. CMT also includes a narrative overview of various aspects of mindfulness meditation practices that are relevant to an emerging-adult college population as well as explorations of cogent aspects of the current mindfulness movement that represent a basic grounding in the various theories, research, and applications in the field. The final chapter and Appendices of the book include a class outline for instructors to be utilized in building their own unique course syllabi as well as a brief bibliography of supportive reading and web resources.

The CMT Semester-Long Protocol

The final chapters of this book lay out a detailed description of activities and recommended course sequencing that can be adapted to either a semester or quarterly academic schedule. Suggestions for adapting the material for individual use, outside of an academic environment, are also included in Chapter 8. Here, I will present a brief outline of the work to suggest a context for CMT within the realms of the other approaches we covered earlier in this chapter.

CMT follows the basic structure of the *College Mindfulness Training* book, including weekly readings, experiential exercises, and class discussions of relevant topics. The class participants in a for-credit class sequence will also document their out-of-class experiential work as well as write reaction papers demonstrating their understanding of certain aspects of the didactic material that is presented both in the book and during classroom lectures. Outside reading material may also be assigned.

In general, the experiential exercise periods recommended for a CMT program run between 20 and 30 minutes, placing the meditation session's length between MBSR and Koru session lengths. When possible, a CMT course sequence will also carry a day-long or half-day silent retreat requirement (very similar to the MBSR requirement). On the whole, the combined experiential and traditional classroom work will be equivalent, in terms of hours required and depth of intellectual engagement, to the average undergraduate or graduate-level university course.

Mindful Movement Exercise

So far, we have primarily been introduced to exercises that focus on single points of attention or movements while standing in place. Now, we will introduce the process of movement to your meditative toolkit by taking up the simple act of walking as our object of attention.

Walking tends to be an automated, unconscious process in our lives. From childhood (with the exception of those that are differently-abled), once the process has been fully learned, people walk without much thought or consciousness of the act at all. Most of the multiple body systems that must be managed in order to walk effectively, such as balance, weight shifting, sensory monitoring of both the limbs and the space around the walker, timing, and muscular control in general, are usually managed by the autonomic nervous system on an unconscious level. After all, if you had to consciously manage every step you took during an average day, you would have a very difficult time getting around at all. However, if we take the act of walking through space as a *subject* of consciousness, we can become re-aware of many of the systems and sensations involved in ambulation, to become "mindful" of an otherwise "mindless" activity.

Walking meditation offers us a very different realm into which we can deploy and discipline our attentional resources. For some people, even after significant disciplined practice, seated, silent meditation forms may be prohibitively difficult. Walking meditation offers an alternative, even if its function and effects may be somewhat different. Second, seated or lying down meditative work can become physically uncomfortable during longer sessions; and so, interspersing walking meditation with passive forms can extend the practitioner's tolerance and capacity for staying focused over progressively longer periods of time. It is common during multi-day meditation retreats, for example, to alternate sessions between seated (passive) and walking (movement) meditations. Also, for most people, walking is a very fundamental act (again, with the exception of those who are differently-abled), making it a commonly shared and widely accessible experience. Walking meditation is an *embodied* form of training as opposed to the more passive aspects of seated meditation (although I would still argue that they are both *active* in important ways). Finally, walking meditation expands the number of types of practice forms we can use, adding some variety and novelty to a CMT training regime.

MINDFUL MOVEMENT—WALKING

Instructions:

No cellphones or digital devices should be present in the room during this exercise, even vibration alerts are distracting. So, power the devices completely off and put them away, out of sight, before the session begins.

Walking as well as all movement exercises are generally best approached wearing loose, comfortable clothing or athletic wear. Where appropriate, this exercise can be done in bare or stocking feet. A direct connection between the feet and the surface of the ground can be useful but is not absolutely necessary.

Locate a space where you can walk at least five to ten paces back and forth without having to avoid or interact with obstacles. As with the other exercise presented so far, walking meditation can be done inside or outside, but it is often best at the beginning to practice in a quiet and secure inside location where distractions and interruptions can be minimized, and everyone can clearly hear the instructions.

If the exercise is to be done in a group, it is best if all participants select a path that will not cross over or interfere with any of the other participants because concentration and focus on your own internally perceived experience is the core of this work. Alternatively, the group can walk in a circle around the perimeter of the room if there is space available, although this will tend to force everyone to adopt a similar tempo.

The exercise is typically done at a fairly slow pace compared to normal daily walking. Slowing the process down, particularly at first, will make it easier to discern the sometimes-subtle movements and shifts in balance that occur during this activity. However, participants should be encouraged to proceed at a pace that is comfortable for them and optimizes their internal awareness of the experience. Slowness is by no means a requirement.

Guidance Script:

Walking meditation begins with standing meditation.

Take a position with feet shoulder-width apart and settle into the chosen spot. Closing the eyes for a moment. (Pause.)

Becoming aware of the body in space. Noticing how the body is balanced on this very spot. Feeling the feet in contact with the floor. Relaxing the body. Standing in alignment, feet relaxed but firmly planted, knees unlocked and slightly bent, pelvis tucked slightly under the torso, spine erect and arms loose at the sides, elbows slightly bent, hands relaxed and fingers slightly curled. You may want to gently roll the shoulders a couple of times, allowing the chest to open as you settle into a relaxed, aligned position.

Now, imagine a string coming out of the top of the head, a balloon attached at the end, gently pulling upwards, helping the body float, spine straight, lengthening, relaxed. (Pause.)

Still with the eyes closed, sense the body on this spot, in relation to gravity, any small movements or swaying that may take place. Take it all in, the sensations of the body simply standing here, in this moment. (Pause.)

And now, let the attention move to the process of breathing. Feel the sensation of coolness at the tips of the nostrils as the breath enters the body and travels through the lungs. Feel the belly rising as the breath fills the body and the chest expands, and now a pause ... before exhalation begins and the process is reversed. Just be with the breath as you stand here, in this moment, centered and calm and relaxed. Fully experience *this* breath ... and *this* breath ... and *this* breath. (Pause.)

Now you may open the eyes. Gaze with a soft focus at the floor a few feet in front of you. Let the attention gather in the feet. And when you are ready, step forward with the right foot, remaining fully present to the experience of raising the foot, swinging it forward through space, and placing it again on the floor. Sense the shift in weight onto the right foot. As your weight shifts, the back foot will roll forward until just the big toe is touching the ground.

Were you able to stay present through the full movement of that one step? Let's try again.

With the left foot this time, raise the foot from the ground, swinging it forward through space, and then shift the weight onto that foot as the back foot rolls forward until just the big toe is touching the ground. Continue walking at your own slowly measured pace for a few steps, keeping the attention fully in the feet as you move across the floor. When you reach the end of the path, carefully pivot, noting where the weight shifts and how the feet feel on the floor as the body turns, staying conscious of every movement. And then walk back to the starting position, attentive to each individual step and its unique qualities. (Pause.)

[Allow the participants to take several steps and to return to their beginning positions. When most participants have completed one lap, continue.]

You may continue the walk, staying mindful of each step, discerning the sensations and changes of balance as they occur. Remember that each step is unique. Savor each step; experience it deeply. (Pause.)

[Participants keep walking.]

If at any time the attention has drifted from the current step, simply acknowledge the thought, or feeling, or memory, or emotion that has captured the attention, and gently but firmly bring the attention back to the very next step you take. Sensing the contact with the floor; the shift in balance; the rolling through of the back foot until only the big toe is touching the ground. [Repeat as necessary.] (Pause.)

[Participants keep walking.]

And now let's try a variation. Allow the attention to stay only with the back foot of each step, so that you carefully experience the rolling through of the foot up onto the big toe; and then when the back foot swings forward through space, let the attention shift onto the other foot as its heel begins to rise from the floor and the contact rolls through the center, onto the ball, and finally through the big toe, and lifts from the ground ... and shift the attention to the new back foot ... so that the attention is always holding on the back foot of the movement as you walk. (Pause.)

[Participants keep walking.]

Now let's shift the attention to the front foot of the walking movement. On the next step forward, allow the attention to focus on the front foot as the heel comes in contact with the ground and the foot plants, weight shifting fully onto the front foot. Try to fully experience the contact with the earth and the pull of gravity as the back foot rises, and then shift the attention to the heel of the other foot as it makes contact and becomes the front foot. Simply keeping the attention on the front foot and its sensations as you continue to walk through space. (Pause.)

[Participants keep walking.]

If at any time you find that the awareness has drifted from the current step, simply acknowledge the thought, or feeling, or memory, or emotion that has captured the attention, and gently but firmly bring attention back to the very next step. Sensing the contact with the floor; keeping the attention on the front foot of each step. [Repeat as necessary.] (Pause.)

[Participants keep walking.]

And now, one more variation. Move the attention into the left foot only and keep it there through the entire walking cycle. Do not shift attention to the right foot, but gently hold it on the left foot as the heel comes in contact with the ground and it becomes the front foot; and stay with it as the weight rolls forward, becoming the back foot again, until only the big toe touches the ground and then rises and swings through space to become the front foot again. Gently stay with the left foot as you continue to walk the path. (Pause.)

[Participants keep walking.]

And now move the attention into the right foot only and keep it there through the entire walking cycle. Do not shift attention to the left foot, but gently hold it on the right foot as the heel comes in contact with the ground and it becomes the front foot. Gently stay with the right foot as you continue to walk your path. (Pause.)

[Participants keep walking.]

When you have returned to your starting place, once again center yourself on both feet, a shoulder-width apart, and come to rest; closing the eyes for a moment. (Pause.)

Becoming aware of the body in space. How does it feel after walking in this way? Noticing how the body is balanced on this very spot. Feeling the feet in contact with the floor. Standing in alignment, feet relaxed but firmly planted, knees unlocked and slightly bent, pelvis tucked slightly under the torso, spine erect and arms loose by the sides, elbows slightly bent, hands relaxed and fingers slightly curled. You may want to gently roll your shoulders a couple of times, allowing the chest to open as the body settles into a relaxed, aligned position.

Allowing the attention to turn towards the breath once more, just breathe for a few moments, savoring each unique breath, centered in *this* moment ... and this moment ... and this moment ... (Pause.)

And when you are ready, slowly and gently, while still maintaining an awareness of the breath, allow awareness to expand to include the room around you, the activity in the space, and the presence of your friends.

Once again, the general goal is to learn the experiential sequence and cultivate an ability to stay with the experience as it unfolds in time, internalizing the exercise and relinquishing the guided version as soon as possible. However, and this applies to all of the guided versions of exercises presented so far, it can be helpful to return, from time to time, to a guided session of the exercises to "check-in" with the process and reinforce the instructions as well as the primary focus of each exercise. This revisiting can also serve as a kind of experiential guidepost for students to evaluate their progress over time. While the instructions are intended to be guidelines only, and there truly is no wrong way to approach these meditative activities as long as focused awareness is at the core, it can simply be helpful to revisit the basics, particularly during a semester-long training, such as in a CMT program.

References

Arnett, J.J. (2000). Emerging adulthood: A theory of development from the late teens through the twenties. *American Psychologist, 55*(5), 469–480. doi:10.1037/0003-066X.55.5.46doi:9

Benson, H. (1975). *The relaxation response.* New York: Morrow.

The Center for Mind-Body Medicine (2018). The Center for Mind-Body Medicine Website. Retrieved from https://cmbm.org/about/mission/.

Davidson, R.J., Goleman, D.J., & Schwartz, G.E. (1976). Attentional and affective concomitants of meditation: A cross-sectional study. *Journal of Abnormal Psychology, 85*(2), 235–238. doi:10.1037/0021-843X.85.2.23doi:5

Goldstein, J. (1976). *The experience of insight: A natural unfolding.* Santa Cruz: Unity Press.

Goleman, D.J., & Schwartz, G.E. (1976). Meditation as an intervention in stress reactivity. *Journal of Consulting and Clinical Psychology, 44*(3), 456–466. doi:10.1037/0022-006X.44.3.45doi:6

Greeson, J.M., Juberg, M.K., Maytan, M., James, K., & Rogers, H. (2014). A randomized controlled trial of Koru: A mindfulness program for college students and other emerging adults. *Journal of American College Health, 62*(4), 222–233. doi:10.1080/07448481.2014.887571

Kabat-Zinn, J. (2011). Some reflections on the origins of MBSR, skillful means, and the trouble with maps. *Contemporary Buddhism, 12*(1), 281–306. doi:10.1080/14639947.2011.564844

Kabat-Zinn, J. (2013). *Full catastrophe living: Using the wisdom of your body and mind to face stress, pain, and illness* (revised and updated edition). New York: Bantam Books.

Kapleau, P. (1966). *The three pillars of Zen: Teaching, practice, and enlightenment* (first US edition). New York: Harper & Row.

Kornfield, J. (1977). *Living Buddhist masters.* Santa Cruz: Unity Press.

Krishnamurti, J. (1969). *Freedom from the known* (first US edition). New York: Harper & Row.

Krishnamurti, J. (1979). *The wholeness of life* (first US edition). San Francisco: Harper & Row.

Nhất, H.N. (1976). *The miracle of mindfulness! A manual of meditation.* Boston: Beacon Press.

Nisargadatta, M. (1973). *I am that.* Bombay: Chetana.

Nyanaponika, T. (1969). *The heart of Buddhist meditation (Satipaṭṭāna): A handbook of mental training based on the Buddha's way of mindfulness, with an anthology of relevant texts translated from the Pali and Sanskrit* (first US edition). New York: Citadel Press.

Page, K. (2018). *Advanced consciousness training for actors: Meditation techniques for the performing artist.* New York: Routledge.

Ramana Maharshi & Osborne, A. (1959). *The collected works of Ramana Maharshi.* London: Rider.

Rogers, H. (2016). *The mindful twenty-something: Life skills to handle stress ... and everything else.* Oakland: New Harbinger Publications.

Rogers, H., & Maytan, M. (2012). *Mindfulness for the next generation: Helping emerging adults manage stress and lead healthier lives.* Oxford and New York: Oxford University Press.

Rogers, H. B. (2018, April 1). Holly Rogers interview by K. Page.

Suzuki, S., & Dixon, T. (1970). *Zen mind, beginner's mind* (first edition). New York: Walker/Weatherhill.

Tart, C.T. (1969). *Altered states of consciousness: A book of readings.* New York: Wiley.

Trungpa, C.G. (1969). *Meditation in action.* London: Stuart & Watkins.

Walsh, R. (1977). Initial meditative experiences part I. *Journal of Transpersonal Psychology*, *9*(2), 151–192.

Walsh, R. (1978). Initial meditative experiences part 2. *Journal of Transpersonal Psychology*, *10*(1), 1–28.

Walsh, R. (1980). The consciousness disciplines and the behavioral sciences: Questions of comparison and assessment. *American Journal of Psychiatry*, *137*(6), 663–673. doi:10.1176/ajp.137.6.66doi:3

Will, A., Rancea, M., Monsef, I., Wöckel, A., Engert, A., & Skoetz, N. (2015). Mindfulness-based stress reduction for women diagnosed with breast cancer. *Cochrane Database of Systematic Reviews*, *2*. doi:10.1002/14651858.CD011518

4

MINDFULNESS IN EVERYDAY LIFE

So far, we have looked primarily at meditation exercises that are performed as discrete activities for a predetermined amount of time. This kind of meditation training activity is often called "formal" practice and represents the core of any kind of attentional training or stress reduction program. Think of formal meditation practice as those times that you explicitly "sit down to meditate." However, as we demonstrated with the "Mindful Eating Exercise #1" in Chapter 1, mindful awareness can also be practiced during the more mundane moments of everyday life, which can be thought of as "informal" practice. Informal practice usually involves purposefully bringing mindful awareness to a common habitual task or series of tasks; examples might include eating, bathing or showering, the process of exercise, etc. Often, it is best to establish some attentional discipline through FAM training before extending the work into the informal domain, however, informal practice can also be a powerful adjunct to formal training of all types in that it allows for the training to be extended into all manner of activities that may be more plentiful and accessible than traditional formal, discrete meditation sessions. Think of informal practice as strengthening or expanding your mindfulness training program by taking the work "beyond the meditation mat."

It is worth noting that a CMT practice will tend to be both *progressive* and *cumulative*. In general, the practice of meditation and its effects tend to grow and unfold along a predictable developmental path. At the beginning of almost any meditation practice (CMT, MBSR, Koru, etc.), it is most common to experience an active, even hyperactive, mind. The thoughts may seem to team and roil like storm clouds or dance around like an excited puppy, as mentioned earlier. This state of consciousness is sometimes characterized as "monkey mind." With practice and repetition, the thoughts will still exist, but they become calmer. Meditation, in one sense, is about watching your own experience and, as you progress, you tend to be less attached to your thoughts; it becomes easier to let them arise and then drift away without being carried away by them. The monkey calms down. However, at the beginning, it is often very difficult to simply stay in the moment of silence and observe thoughts as they arise and pass. Instead, many beginning meditators struggle with their own thinking and are often distracted or carried away with one fantasy or another. *This is normal.* Be assured, if you keep at it, your practice (and your control over it) will grow and deepen along a generally predictable path.

While the effect or results of any single formal meditation session may be frustrating or disappointing in many different ways, it is the cumulative effects over time that are of most use for attentional training, stress management, and creativity. You may not notice any particular effect from an individual seated mediation session, for instance, but do it every day for three months without fail and you will definitely notice a change in your overall consciousness: a "loosening" of consciousness, an enhanced ability to focus attention and to be still in the present moment. In addition, the meditator may start to recognize some qualitative difference in consciousness and perspective; looking at things in a different way, more creative thinking, a more pliable imagination, and such.

By extending the number of moments we utilize mindful awareness during the day (formal or informal), we leverage the progressive and cumulative properties of a wholistic CMT practice and speed our progress through the sequence. There are numerous examples of opportunities where we can cultivate a state of mindful awareness in our everyday lives; I will present only a few below. The clever student will compose numerous other creative ways to practice mindfulness in the specific circumstances of their own lives (perhaps mindfully doing the dishes or mindfully putting on socks and shoes?).

Mindful Eating Exercise #2

As noted in Chapter 1, one of the most common human activities is eating. In many cases, eating is habitual and done with little awareness beyond filling the overriding goal of quenching physical hunger. In Western culture, we often hurry through our meals with little consciousness awareness of what we are doing. In Chapter 1 we introduced the Mindful Eating Exercise #1 which focuses on a single bite-sized morsel of food explored in a mindful fashion. Below, we will extend this activity to include an entire meal consumed in a mindful fashion.

MINDFUL EATING EXERCISE #2

Instructions:
   Prepare your meal and place it on a table or tray before you. Sit comfortably but erect. If you normally slouch at the dining table, you might

consider sitting on the front edge of the chair with your body aligned and your back relatively straight as in a seated meditation posture. The idea is to be comfortable but alert throughout the dining experience without the need to shift or change positions often, so that the focus can remain on the act of eating.

Take a few moments to settle into your seat and become present to the moment. You might bring your attention to the breath for a few cycles.

Take in the food before you. Observe the colors of the food. Is there steam coming off any of the items? What aromas do you smell? Are there any sensations in your body as you gaze upon the meal you are about to partake of? Are you salivating? Is your stomach grumbling? Do you have the sensation of hunger? Take in the sounds of the room. Fully open yourself to your senses before you begin to eat. How does it feel just before you take your first bite of food?

Take your time and luxuriate in the sensuality of the act of eating food.

Slowly and mindfully pick up an eating utensil or piece of food, as appropriate. Experience the muscles in your arm and hand as you reach forward and grasp the item. If you have picked up a fork or spoon, explore it for a moment. Turn it over in your hand. What are its qualities? Weight? Does it sparkle in the light?

If you have picked up a food item, explore it in the same way. What is the texture of the food item? Does it bend? Is it spongy? Look at it from all angles. Can you discover anything about this food item that you have never noticed before? Does it make a sound when held close to your ear? Perhaps touch it to your cheek or your lips without opening your mouth. What is the texture on your skin? Explore the item thoroughly before you begin eating.

Check in with your body and your breath. Are there any sensations of anticipation? Take in the sounds and any activity in your surroundings. Be fully present to *this* moment just before placing food in your mouth.

Place the first bite of food in your mouth, but do not begin chewing yet. Simply sense the food on your tongue. What is the temperature and texture? Is it juicy or dry? How does your body react to having food in the mouth and not chewing? What is the experience of taste *before* you begin to chew?

If you used an eating utensil to place the food in your mouth, set it back down on the table and place your hands in your lap. Relax and bring your full attention to the act of beginning to chew the food. Chew slowly and deliberately. Try to experience each chewing motion as unique. Observe any changes in the sensations in your mouth as the bite of food is chewed. Experience the flavor as it is unlocked in the act of chewing. When it is time to swallow, do it deliberately. What is the sensation of swallowing like? Is the food swallowed all at once? Or is it done in a sequence? Finish the entire chewing and swallowing cycle before picking up your eating utensil and starting again.

> If it is time to take a drink of a beverage, bring the same level of mindfulness to the activity as you did with the food. Note the muscular mechanics of picking up the glass, the sensations before opening your mouth to take a sip, the sensations in your mouth as you take in the liquid, the flavors and sense of wetness on your tongue, and finally the swallowing of the beverage. Finish each drink completely and fully before moving on to the next.
>
> Continue the meal in this fashion until you are full and the meal has been completed.

Mindful eating and other informal exercises like it (see below) can be combined with a disciplined regime of formal exercises to extend and leverage your mindful moments throughout the day, taking full advantage of the cumulative qualities of meditation practice described earlier. Many people will initially claim they have little time in their rushed daily schedules for regular CMT work; however, by carefully using a menu of informal mindful exercises combined with more formal FAM and OMM work, sometimes in short intervals at multiple times during the day, a significant CMT practice can be executed with very little schedule disruption or change. As with anything of significance, the importance imbued upon the work itself and *the intention with which it is engaged* will often determine its actual viability more than a cursory and superficial dismissal. Establishing a successful CMT practice entails mindful decisions and choices.

Mindful Bathing

Another regular activity that tends to be mostly habitual is bathing or showering. Ask yourself when was the last time that you were fully aware, in a conscious, embodied way, through an entire morning shower? Most people will admit that they move through their regular ritual of daily self-care with little or no conscious awareness to the details of the experience, making bathing a perfect avenue for mindfulness practice. As with eating, bathing is an activity that takes place regularly and is something that everyone does, making it an easily accessible activity.

> **MINDFUL BATHING EXERCISE**
>
> Instructions:
> Prepare either the water in a bathtub or adjust the shower to a comfortable temperature. Remove all clothing and jewelry before you begin.
>
> Take a moment to center yourself before entering the water. You may want to tune in to your breath for a few beats and experience the space and sounds and odors of the bathing chamber.
>
> Enter the tub or shower stall slowly. Experience the first contact of the water with your skin. What does that feel like? How is the temperature

> different from that of the air in the room around you? Do you notice any sensations in other areas of your body? As the water envelops your body, luxuriate in the sensuality of the act of bathing.
>
> Once you are fully submerged in the bath or beneath the stream from the shower head, take a moment to scan your entire body. What is the sensation of being submerged or being "rained on?" Notice the sensation of being wet and try to discover qualities of this experience that you may have never noticed before. What are the sounds of the water? Is there steam rising around you? What does the water smell like? Fully experience the water on your flesh before moving on.
>
> Once you have become fully present to the experience of the water on your skin, take a bar of soap or wash cloth and begin cleansing yourself in a wholly present way, noting each sensation and discovering things you might normally miss. Pay particular attention to the sounds and smells during the entire cleaning process.
>
> Continue bathing and rinsing, staying mindful and present to the entire process until complete. Take extra care when exiting the tub or shower area to avoid accidents.
>
> Continue to track the experience in every detail you can through the drying off process. What is the feeling of the towel? Which parts of your body do you dry first? Try to become aware of the component parts of this activity and their order during this commonly habitual activity. What does the towel smell like? How does it feel against your skin? Does the texture of the towel feel different when rubbing different parts of the body? Continue mindfully until you are dry and ready to get dressed.

From these few examples of informal mindful activities, you should be able to extend the practice to almost any activity during your day. The very nature of mindfulness invites such practices and indeed the act of becoming mindful of activities that were once mostly unconscious can become a joy of discovery. Mindfulness is portable; leverage that fact in your own practice. There is literally no experience that cannot be observed with a mindful eye.

Mindfulness of Technology

As noted in Chapter 2, there is much research to support the idea that technology use, in general, and mobile digital media multi-tasking, in particular, are causing widespread symptoms of distraction and consciousness fragmentation that are particularly troublesome for the college student and emerging adult. One of the strategies to counteract the effects of this wave of mass-distraction is to moderate behavior related to mobile technology use by becoming more aware of the circumstances and internal drives around the act of technology use. To the degree that technology use has become habitual and "mindless," then technology has also become a viable object for mindful investigation. This can be approached in a number of ways.

Reaching for a cellphone to check texts, phone messages, or social media feeds is often an activity that is done compulsively, without much mindful engagement (in a similar way to gobbling down food or speeding through a daily shower). This compulsive mediation of experience through technology can interfere with interpersonal relationships and attention spans, and has even been implicated in causing, or at least predicting, moods of depression, social anxiety, and disrupting well-being (Becker, Alzahabi, & Hopwood, 2013; Cain & Mitroff, 2011; Gorman & Green, 2016; Lepp, Barkley, & Karpinski, 2014; Sriwilai & Charoensukmongkol, 2015). Some studies have indicated that mindfulness practices can help ameliorate these effects (Gazzaley & Rosen, 2016; Levy, Wobbrock, Kaszniak, & Ostergren, 2012; Mrazek, Franklin, Phillips, Baird, & Schooler, 2013; Mrazek, Smallwood, & Schooler, 2012). Very often in college-level classes students will log onto or engage a mobile device immediately upon the conclusion of class *rather than interact with classmates or faculty* who are present in the room. This is what is meant by the "mediation" of experience through a technological platform; a preference or favoring for filtering social interactions through technology rather than directly with other individuals. The use of this technology can probably not be thwarted, nor its negative effects fully denuded, but *awareness* can be brought to bear on the worst of the behavior through the simple application of informal mindfulness practice.

One approach the individual student might consider would be the limiting or excluding of mobile digital technology from the better part of the school day, especially between classes. It is best to fully power down digital devices and put them out of sight, such as in a locker or closed backpack. Part of the reason for this is that even the presence of these devices, when out of reach but turned on, has been shown to create anxiety and distraction (Cheever, Rosen, Carrier, & Chavez, 2014). Instead, use the time between classes to talk and interact with your fellow students and faculty. Perhaps pause for a few moments of mindfulness before moving on to the next task.

If you find yourself strongly resisting the foregoing advice, ask yourself why? Can you become mindful of the need and its level of urgency to dive into the virtual world of your cellphone instead of interacting with others? Perhaps you have a fear of "missing out" (Przybylski, Murayama, DeHaan, & Gladwell, 2013)? If you find that you have an addiction to mobile digital technology, it is perhaps worth redoubling your efforts to use the technology more mindfully (Gorman & Green, 2016; Sriwilai & Charoensukmongkol, 2015).

You might try structuring or mindfully reducing your cellphone usage in similar ways, perhaps choosing to check in only at preset times during the day or making more conscious choices about when and how often you do so. Anxiety related to your devices or computer may be indicating less-than-mindful attachments that perhaps should be dealt with proactively (Gazzaley & Rosen, 2016).

Another approach to cultivating mindfulness around personal technology use might be to take an occasional weekend retreat from technology in which you unplug for a preset period of time and deploy your attention in more traditional ways. (Perhaps a silent mini-retreat? See below.)

Try putting aside two hours every day (much of which may be used for your CMT session work) where you fully disengage from your devices. This could in part be accomplished, for instance, by refraining from music or other digital content during physical exercise, informal mindfulness exercises with phones off, or as part of your formal CMT exercises, which are always performed with technology powered down. The simple addition of conscious, purposeful non-screen time during your day may help bring your digital behavior into consciousness and start to ameliorate symptoms of distraction and overuse.

In any situation, try to engage technology more mindfully; be aware of the impulse to check in, what it feels like when you think you are missing out, what it feels like to delay the urge for five minutes. Consciously engage in a live conversation instead of checking your phone. What may seem like a hindrance or a challenge at first may begin to grow into useful insight and a heightened ability to *choose* where you place and direct your attention. In this way, mindfulness of technology becomes another aspect of informal CMT.

The Silent Mini-Retreat

In most traditional schools of meditation training there is provided some form of "silent retreat" for the deepening of the practice and the intensifying of the effects over a short but concentrated period of time. The silent retreat, in a general sense, is an extended period set aside for intensive meditation practice and self-observation of that practice's effects upon consciousness. Silent retreats can last for any amount of time, from a half-day (as will be detailed below) to multiple weeks and even months for the very advanced practitioner. The essential difference between daily meditation practice and a silent retreat experience is in the "dosage" of the meditation and the constant focus of attention even between formal sessions on mindful awareness. This higher dosage combined with constant focus of attention will tend to amplify the effects of the meditation and often lead to insights or creative bursts in the meditator's consciousness.

For the most part, the exercises introduced in this book so far are intended to last between 20 and 30 minutes per session, with the possible extension throughout the day of added informal practice time (also in increments of half an hour or less). This 30-minute average session length falls in between the average session length of 45 minutes to an hour for MBSR exercises and the ten to 20 minutes a day for Koru training. This average session length generally places CMT training protocols at the "modest beginner" level of practice. However, with the addition of occasional silent retreat experiences, the CMT student has the opportunity to solidify their experiential understanding of the state of mindfulness and possibly deepen their self-observation and understanding. Therefore, the occasional (guided where possible) silent retreat is a strongly recommended part of any CMT program, particularly if it is part of a semester-long class at the university level.

The typical silent retreat is structured in an environment where a group (or the individual) can fully engage with the meditation practice in a safe and protected environment. Usually, all meals, and even sleeping arrangements, in the case of multi-day retreats, are pre-arranged. A quiet and secure space is reserved for the formal meditation sessions where the group can sit or walk together in uninterrupted silence for the duration of the retreat event. Upon arrival at the retreat location, participants will store their bags or supplies and prepare to enter the experience, often through a formal ceremony or introductory session where the rules for the retreat are explained. After the introduction, all participants enter total vocal silence for the duration of the retreat which includes an abstinence of eye contact or any other kind of social engagement. The restriction on eye contact or otherwise engaging other participants is to relieve all members of the group of the responsibility of social engagements, so that even though the retreat may be taken in a group setting, the individual can concentrate fully on silently engaging in the practice of both meditation and contemplation. It is often surprising to people how potent this communal silence can be in strengthening the experience and intensity of meditation. While most of us are very accustomed to spending time interacting with different groups of people in society, it is very rare to spend a significant amount of time in a group where all are in a state of concentrated silence.

The course of events and styles of practice engaged may vary depending on the style or school of meditation training that is offering the retreat, but on the whole, speech and social interactions are reduced to an absolute minimum, the primary activities throughout the day are meditation-based exercises, all meals are taken in silence (and usually consumed in a mindful fashion, making the taking of meals another form of practice). There is no television or any other kind of media allowed during the retreat duration, this typically will include reading of books or listening to recorded lectures. The formal silence is respected throughout the course of the event, even on break periods and throughout all waking hours (if it is a multi-day experience). The only exception to the silence rule is during any formal meeting with a teacher or retreat leader which may be arranged in a private room that will not disturb the other participants. During these formal teacher/student meetings, participants are allowed to ask questions or discuss their experiences with the qualified leader (often someone with years of practical experiential meditation training themselves).

The typical session structure during a retreat day might consist of an early morning silent seated meditation (anywhere between 30 minutes and two hours), a silent breakfast where participants concentrate on the experiences of the eating process, a morning session of between two and three hours of meditation practice (often a combination of seated and movement exercises), followed by a silent lunch and perhaps a break period where participants are invited to walk in nature or otherwise relax in contemplative silence. A similar afternoon session of practice may or may not be followed with a brief talk by the instructor. Dinner is held, once again, in silent contemplation of the process of eating and then either an evening session or silent free time before bed.

As you can see from this general description, the silence and extension of practice into the full hours of a day will most likely be far more intense and captivating than a short 20–30-minute session held during a break from a "normal" school day. For any silent retreat session over eight hours, the presence of a qualified instructor is highly recommended if not required. A higher dose than eight hours of continuous silent meditation can potentially cause strong altered states of consciousness and should only be attempted under supervision. With that caution in mind, I will present an outline for a half-day (four-hour) silent "mini retreat" than can be used as a model for a group retreat experience or as an individual retreat experience that can be done in the privacy of your home or any other safe location that you have access to where you won't be distracted or interrupted for a minimum of four hours.

A FOUR-HOUR SILENT MINI-RETREAT

Pre-arrange a space where you will be safe and uninterrupted for a period of four hours. Turn off and remove all mobile digital devices from the space. There should be no TVs, radios, or any other type of information devices (including books) in the space. If you are in a group, these instructions should be explained and an agreement for total silence between group members committed to by all participants. This includes eye contact or any other type of social interaction that requires communication or response. It is important to respect each other's commitment to silence along with your own during this time.

The first session of the day is a 30-minute body scan meditation (see Chapter 1). If done in a group of relative novices, a group leader can be elected to read the guidance script or a pre-recorded version of the guidance can be used. If the retreat is for an individual alone, either simply internalize the instructions and silently guide yourself through the body scan or use a pre-recorded version of the guidance (this is the one variance on the ban of electronic devices).

After the initial body scan, there can be a 10–15-minute walking meditation (see Chapter 3). In addition to creating a slightly different meditative experience (focusing attention on the movement process rather than discreet parts of the body), it will also help to relieve any stiffness or numbness associated with lying down or sitting still for long periods.

Next is a 30-minute seated meditation concentrating on the process of breathing. Depending on the experience level of the practitioners, they may count or label their breathes (silently to themselves), or, if it is a beginner's

> group, the session can be lead using a guidance script (see Chapter 2—FAM on the Breath).
>
> As with all of the seated or lying down meditation sessions throughout the retreat, this 30-minute session is followed by a 10–15-minute movement meditation, either walking (Chapter 3) or Conscious Breathing (Chapter 1).
>
> Sessions of seated (or lying down depending on personal preference) meditation (FAM on the Breath) are alternated with the two movement-oriented meditations for the next several cycles.
>
> A break (still in silence) may be included as appropriate. However, during any breaks, it is important to remind the participants to remain committed to mindful silence, which includes complete abstinence from all cellphones and electronic media. The content of any breaks should remain focused on individual's conscious experience in the present moment and distractions should be avoided. The break may also include a snack (taken in silence) that is consumed as an informal mindfulness of eating exercise.
>
> The final sessions of the day should consist of Open Monitoring Meditation (OMM) or mindfulness (see instructions below) and a final movement meditation sequence, either walking or conscious breathing.
>
> At the end of the four-hour retreat, if it has been a group activity, a formal breaking of the silence occurs, and the group members may wish to discuss their individual experiences. If this has been a solo effort, the student may want to take a half an hour to journal any feelings or responses they had to the experience, before rejoining the activities of the outside world.

Silent retreat experiences, even in durations as short as four hours as described above, can be very fruitful events and help solidify and advance a program of CMT. In a way, a retreat is like the final application of a skill that has been practiced for many months; like a baseball game or other sport where practice is required to master the fundamentals before the actual sport is engaged in competition.

Before moving on to more advance applications of meditation practice, we still need to introduce the culmination of the practices we have learned and applied thus far. And so, with a grounding in the basic FAM techniques we have already explored, we now introduce *Open Monitoring Meditation* (OMM), which differs from FAM practices in that we now take all of our experience as objects of awareness in the present moment instead of focusing on a very limited set of inputs (such as the process of breathing or walking).

OMM or Mindfulness Meditation Practice

In order to introduce this exercise for actual practice, I will provide a set of explicit instructions and a guided script equivalent to those in previous exercises.

Although the initial instructions and beginning of the exercise are almost identical to what you have seen before, the instructions will be restated for the convenience of the group leader or narrator. However, it should be noted again that the scripted version is only intended to be used as an introduction to the practice and a learning tool for the formal instructions, and the instructions should be internalized as soon as is practical for the individual student. Also, as you have most likely been practicing the general methods of these exercises for some time by now, the transition from a fixed object of attention (FAM) to experience in general as the object (OMM) should be fairly smooth and rapid in comparison to the initial training sequences.

OPEN MONITORING MEDITATION (OMM) OR MINDFULNESS PRACTICE

Instructions:

No cellphones or digital devices should be present in the room during this exercise, even vibration alerts are distracting. So, power the devices completely off and put them away, out of sight, before the session begins.

Sit on the floor on a cushion or mat and use a meditation pillow to elevate your buttocks slightly above your knees (if you are sitting cross-legged). You can also sit on a chair with your feet on the ground in front of you, shoulder-width apart. Place your hands palms up in your lap, right hand cradling left, with thumb tips lightly touching. Your hands and arms should be relaxed. You can also place your hands palms down on your thighs. Once you've found your position, settle in and allow your awareness to turn inward.

You can also lie on the floor for this exercise. You may want to use a yoga mat and some low pillows to support your neck and slightly raise the knees. Place your hands comfortably at your sides, palms either up or down. Hands can also be draped lightly on top of your abdomen but avoid interlocking the fingers. The goal is to remain comfortably in this position for half an hour or more without the need to overly shift or adjust your position. Relaxation will be an integral part of this practice.

This exercise can also be done in a standing position. Center yourself over your feet which should be shoulder-width apart. Keep your feet relaxed but firmly planted, knees unlocked and slightly bent, pelvis tucked slightly under your torso, spine erect and arms loose at your sides with palms turned naturally in towards the thighs, your elbows slightly bent, hands relaxed and fingers slightly curled. You may want to gently roll your shoulders a couple of times, allowing the chest to open as you settle into a relaxed, aligned position. Again, the goal is to remain comfortably in this position for half an hour or more without the need to overly shift or adjust your position.

While you can close your eyes, I recommend keeping them open and softly focused. If you are seated, you can let your eyelids droop slightly and pick a spot on the floor between three and five feet in front of you, where you can focus without straining. Again, you want a soft focus so that while individual objects may be slightly blurred, you are still able to see the objects in your immediate field of vision. If you are lying down, pick an area of the ceiling (or sky) that you can gaze upon easily without staring. The point is to *stay awake and alert* for the duration of the exercise without falling asleep or causing tension in the eyes. If you choose to close your eyes, be warned that this often can lead to sleep, which is not our goal. If you find yourself drifting out of consciousness, you may want to open your eyes, blink a few times, and maintain a soft focus as you continue.

Unless you otherwise cannot, due to blocked airways or the like, it is recommended that you keep your mouth closed during all meditation exercises and *breathe through your nose*. While your mouth is closed, allow your tongue to rest, pressed gently against the front teeth. This will prevent excessive salivation and swallowing which can be a distraction during an extended session.

Guidance Script:

Take a moment to settle into the body. Release any tensions and allow awareness to focus on breathing.

Simply experience the body breathing for the next five breaths. (Pause.)

Continue to release any tensions that may arise while the attention is turned inward.

Allow the attention to focus on the *sensation* of breathing. As each breath enters the body, notice the coolness at the tip of the nostrils where the air enters. Experience that sensation of coolness completely.

As each breath enters the body, it makes a journey, from the nose down through the chest, where it expands the belly with life-giving air. Follow the path of the next breath as it makes its journey ... first in at the nostrils, then expanding the belly, then filling the chest. There is a pause ... and then the chest begins to fall and the belly contract as the exhalation cycle begins. (Pause.)

Follow this entire process, being fully aware of each sensation, for the next few breath cycles. (Pause.)

And now, let the awareness expand to include the sensations of the body. Experience just being a body. Track any sensations you might find? Hot or cold? Any tingling or places of numbness. Aches or pains? Whatever sensations are there, just acknowledge them, perhaps give them a label: "Coolness. Numbness. Aching. Tingling." Whatever is there, in awareness of the body, just allow it to enter consciousness, label it, and then gently let it go without judgment. (Pause.)

And now, let the awareness expand to include the sense of smell. Are there any subtle aromas in the air around you? Can you smell your own cologne or perfume? Body odor? Are there other scents in the air? Just be with the sense of smell for a while and if you identify a smell, simply label it, in a non-judgmental way; and then let it go, as you continue to inhabit this space at this moment. (Pause.)

And now, let the awareness expand to include any sounds you might hear in the room ... the sound of the air conditioner ... the sound of the floor or the walls creaking ... the sound of your friends breathing around you ... sounds coming from outside of the room. Just take in any sounds that happen to be present. Gently acknowledge them, perhaps give them a label, and then let them go. (Pause.)

And now, let the awareness expand to include the entire room, whatever sensations might be present in *this* very room at *this* very moment, just be with those sensations for a moment. Be alive in *this* moment ... in *this* room. And any sensations or thoughts or feelings that might arise, simply acknowledge them, perhaps give them a simple one or two-word label, and then let them float on by with the next moment ... which becomes *this* present moment of time, with its unique sensory and mental impressions. Just be with us here ... be with us now ... in this very moment, whatever it brings. And now, simply rest here in the present, open to whatever sensation or feeling or thought or memory might arise ... and continue to breathe and experience the silence. (Pause.)

And, if at any time, the mind has wandered away from awareness of the present moment, gently acknowledge the sensation, thought, memory, or emotion that has captured the attention, and let it go, without judgment, and allow the attention to return to *this* present moment in *this* very room. [Repeat as necessary.] (Pause.)

[Participants continue to meditate for the duration of the session.]

And now, slowly and gently, when you are ready, allow the awareness to re-inhabit the body and your own individual breath. Take a few moments to simply breathe as you come back to the activity in the room and the presence of your friends.

This is the basic OMM or mindfulness meditation practice, where any experience that arises, mental or physical sensation, momentarily becomes the object of attention before being gently acknowledged and then let go. It is consciousness becoming aware of *itself* in each successive present moment. It may take some practice to let go of the various objects of attention, such as breath or other sensations, that you have been focusing on with such intensity in your earlier practice and simply let awareness be aware; but with time, mindfulness practice will become one of the most powerful CMT exercises in your toolkit.

As explained earlier, you should internalize the instructions as soon as is practical and make mindfulness meditation a main core practice that is entered into through the breath and then followed into each successive moment of the session.

In core practice, the individual directions for mindfulness practice found in the scripted version are dropped and awareness is simply followed for awareness's sake: mindfully, in the moment, just so; your very being will provide the content.

If OMM is too difficult to maintain, after a reasonable period of effort, you can return to FAM practice until you develop your attentional function enough to stay with pure experience without a particular object. A skilled meditation teacher will be able to advise you on when it is best to start making this transition to including mindfulness practice in your regime.

One of the most important qualities of a state of open awareness or mindfulness consciousness is that of *non-attachment*. When practicing and thus experiencing open awareness, the objects that arise in consciousness (feelings, thoughts, memories, physical objects and sensations, both internal to the body and external via sensorial data) are merely observed with what is often called "bare attention," meaning they are observed and acknowledged but not imbued with any additional significance or emotional weight. The objects of open awareness are not mentally attached to nor identified with, but merely observed in a completely non-judgmental way. They are neither good nor bad, they simply *are* at their moment of arising.

References

Becker, M.W., Alzahabi, R., & Hopwood, C.J. (2013). Media multitasking is associated with symptoms of depression and social anxiety. *Cyberpsychology, Behavior, and Social Networking, 16*(2), 132–135.

Cain, M.S., & Mitroff, S.R. (2011). Distractor filtering in media multitaskers. *Perception, 40*(10), 1183–1192.

Cheever, N.A., Rosen, L.D., Carrier, L.M., & Chavez, A. (2014). Out of sight is not out of mind: The impact of restricting wireless mobile device use on anxiety levels among low, moderate and high users. *Computers in Human Behavior, 37*, 290–297. doi:10.1016/j.chb.2014.05.002

Gazzaley, A., & Rosen, L.D. (2016). *The distracted mind: Ancient brains in a high-tech world.* Cambridge, MA: MIT Press.

Gorman, T.E., & Green, C.S. (2016). Short-term mindfulness intervention reduces the negative attentional effects associated with heavy media multitasking. *Scientific Reports, 6*, 24542. doi:10.1038/srep24542. Retrieved from www.nature.com/articles/srep24542/.

Lepp, A., Barkley, J.E., & Karpinski, A.C. (2014). The relationship between cell phone use, academic performance, anxiety, and satisfaction with life in college students. *Computers in Human Behavior, 31*, 343–350.

Levy, D.M., Wobbrock, J.O., Kaszniak, A.W., & Ostergren, M. (2012). The effects of mindfulness meditation training on multitasking in a high-stress information environment. Paper presented at the Proceedings of Graphics Interface 2012, Toronto, Ontario, Canada.

Mrazek, M.D., Franklin, M.S., Phillips, D.T., Baird, B., & Schooler, J.W. (2013). Mindfulness training improves working memory capacity and GRE performance while reducing mind wandering. *Psychological Science, 241*(5), 776–781.

Mrazek, M.D., Smallwood, J., & Schooler, J.W. (2012). Mindfulness and mind-wandering: Finding convergence through opposing constructs. *Emotion*, *12*(3), 442–448.

Przybylski, A.K., Murayama, K., DeHaan, C.R., & Gladwell, V. (2013). Motivational, emotional, and behavioral correlates of fear of missing out. *Computers in Human Behavior*, *29*(4), 1841–1848.

Sriwilai, K., & Charoensukmongkol, P. (2015). Face it, don't Facebook it: Impacts of social media addiction on mindfulness, coping strategies and the consequence on emotional exhaustion. *Stress and Health*, *32*, 427–434.

5
MIND/BODY FITNESS

According to a cover story published by the American Psychological Association (APA), the largest professional association of psychologists in the world, in *Monitor on Psychology* (December 2011, Vol 42, No. 11) "the exercise-mental health connection is becoming impossible to ignore." Research studies have provided solid evidence of exercise's positive effects on anxiety (Daley, 2002; Smits et al., 2008), depression (Fox, 1999; Gerber, Holsboer-Trachsler, Pühse, & Brand, 2016), and cognitive brain function in both the young and old (Cotman & Berchtold, 2002; Cox et al., 2016; Erickson et al., 2010, 2011; Fabel & Kempermann, 2008). These are significant findings for college-aged emerging adults, as we pointed out in Chapter 1 that the majority of mental health complaints acknowledged by college students are anxiety (particularly around cognitive performance and stress) and depression. Similarly, nutrition now is being acknowledged for its role in mood and well-being (Jacka, Cherbuin, Anstey, Sachdev, & Butterworth, 2015; Lai et al., 2014; O'Neil et al., 2013, 2014; Sarris et al., 2015). So, while it may seem odd to discuss exercise and nutrition as part of a systematized program of college mindfulness training, the evidence supports the notion that nutrition and physical fitness may in fact be important components or even prerequisites to a stable mindfulness program.

As a college professor of theater once explained to me:

> Students will sometimes come to my office, almost in tears, complaining that they can hardly function for the level of stress they feel they are under. When I ask them how much sleep they got the night before, they reply "I don't know; maybe two or three hours? But I'll take a nap this afternoon." Then, when I ask what they've had to eat that day, they say something like

"a couple of pop tarts." So, to me, it is no wonder they are feeling stressed and overwhelmed!

(Utterback, 2017)

Basic self-care is an important foundation of a mindfulness program and a basic sense of well-being. Proper amounts of sleep (Hamilton, Nelson, Stevens, & Kitzman, 2007; Kalak, Lemola, Brand, Holsboer-Trachsler, & Grob, 2014), a reasonable diet, with limited sweets and junk foods (Jacka et al., 2015; O'Neil et al., 2014), and a regular exercise program can make a significant impact on a student's mood, sense of well-being, and resilience under stress (Cox et al., 2016; Edwards & Loprinzi, 2018; Fox, 1999; Kelly et al., 2018; Pontifex et al., 2011; Themanson, Pontifex, & Hillman, 2008; Walsh, 2011). The American College of Sports Medicine recommends a minimum of 150 minutes of moderate-intensity exercise per week (Donnelly et al., 2009). However, only about 20% of Americans actually get that amount of combined cardiovascular and strength training in their daily lives. Furthermore, people with a sedentary lifestyle with low or no regular physical exercise run higher risks of serious diseases like cancer, heart disease, and Alzheimer's.

Becoming mindfully aware of diet and exercise habits can be useful tools for dealing with the stresses and anxieties of college life. There have even been studies that looked at affective improvements from doses of exercise and meditation combined (Edwards & Loprinzi, 2018), which we will look at more closely in a section below. However, to begin with, all CMT students that are taking a serious interest in developing a mindfulness practice should consider taking up an exercise program that combines aerobic and strength-training sessions for a minimum total of 150 minutes per week as part of their program. Another resource is the book *Exercise for Mood and Anxiety: Proven Strategies for Overcoming Depression and Enhancing Well-Being*, in which psychologists Michael Otto and Jasper Smits detail a number of useful strategies for integrating exercise into your life for stress management and general self-care (Otto & Smits, 2011). If you have been previously sedentary or are otherwise starting to exercise for the first time, you should check with your personal physician to make sure you do not have any health restrictions or limitations before beginning.

Mindful Exercise

Many college students may already be involved in a physical fitness routine. However, it is also common practice to utilize music or other digitally delivered content to occupy the mind while doing the physical work of a workout. Often, when people do this, they argue that they are trying to "stave off boredom" or other similar justifications. Interestingly enough, boredom is defined as "the state of being weary and restless through lack of interest," which is in most cases a function of not being engaged with the current circumstance or activity. However, to the degree that we engage directly and intently (one might say mindfully) in the activity at hand, boredom tends to evaporate. Technically, if you are listening to music or a book-on-tape while jogging or otherwise working out in a gym, you are multi-tasking (as discussed in Chapter 2) and doing your workout in a "mindless" manner. So, CMT would suggest a different way to approach your workout routine.

Mantra as a Point of Meditative Focus

So far, we have primarily introduced forms of FAM that utilize bodily functions (breathing, etc.) or physical processes (such as slow, concentrated walking) as their point of focus. The one exception has been the OMM or mindfulness exercise introduced at the end of the last chapter where all experience became the focus of attention as those experiences arise in consciousness. Now, we will introduce a different kind of object of attention called a "mantra," which uses a word or phrase as its focal point. Using a mantra for meditative focus offers a number of unique benefits, not the least of which is that you can apply it to other sorts of activities than breathing or sensory processes, thus expanding the types of activities that can be used for meditation and mindfulness practice.

Traditional mantra meditations can be found in almost every major religious or spiritual tradition from around the world, including Christianity, Judaism, Islam, Buddhism, and Hinduism (Bormann, 2010, p. 85; Goleman, 1988, p. 186). The basic idea is to pick a word or simple phrase and repeat it over and over again, focusing the attention on that word or phrase as the exclusive subject of awareness during the session. In mantra practice, the mantra can be repeated either silently or vocalized as a type of chant. We will look primarily at ways to apply the silent version. Because the focus of attention is on an internalized word or phrase, it allows us to work with the mantra "beyond the meditation mat" in numerous informal ways.

The word "mantra" comes from ancient Sanskrit words that translate into English as "mind" and "to set free or protect from." Therefore, one possible definition for the term mantra is "to set free from the mind"; another could be "the thought that liberates or protects" (Bormann, 2010, p. 79). Regardless of technical definition, CMT practices based on mantra repetition can be powerful tools for cultivating the attention function. Mantra practice is "portable" and can be utilized as a very brief "check-in" activity that, particularly over time, can help to strengthen the general attention function (Bormann, 2010, pp. 83–85).

For many years, mantra meditation was perhaps the best-known form of meditation practice in the West as a result of the popularization of Transcendental Meditation (TM) by that movement's founder, Maharishi Mahesh Yogi, an Indian mystic who toured the United States and Europe extensively, promoting his particular brand of mantra repetition practice (Goldberg, 2010; Mason, 1994). Today, there has been a great surge in the interest and popularity of mindfulness meditation practices, and now it is difficult to judge which approach is most popular in the West. In CMT, we integrate both approaches.

TM is a Westernized version of Vedic meditation for "householders" (non-monastic practitioners), based on mantra repetition. The Vedas are ancient Indian spiritual teachings that form the basis for Hinduism, parts of which arose as early as 1700 BCE, and are the source of yoga, ayurvedic medicine, and the type of meditation that Siddhartha (The Buddha) drew from and practiced before founding Buddhism sometime between the 6th and 4th centuries BCE. In TM, meditators are given a mantra chosen especially for them by a qualified TM teacher. TM mantras are selected from a list of traditional Sanskrit words that have been used by Hindus for thousands of years. The general approach toward meditation in TM, as it is in mantra repetition practice in CMT, is to avoid effortful concentration and to instead bring the mind gently back to the mantra when it wanders. By repeatedly and consistently leading the mind back to the mantra repetition, the meditator cultivates a "focal narrowing of attention" that eventually stabilizes the mind and brings a general clarity to consciousness, called by the Maharishi "cosmic consciousness" (Goleman, 1988, pp. 68–69).

Selecting a Basic Mantra

There are many sources for mantras. As mentioned above, you can have a Vedic or certified TM teacher select one for you. Or, you can simply pick a word or phrase that has positive or neutral meaning for you. You might do a simple Internet search and see what others have used as mantras. Avoid terms that carry a strong emotional charge, as the goal is to enter a state of focused concentration more than to contemplate a specific mental construct or idea. It is often useful to keep a mantra very simple and to perhaps pick a word or phrase more for its tonal qualities than its explicit meaning. Once you have settled on a particular word or phrase for your mantra, you are encouraged to stick with it and resist changing it, at least for a significant period of time. The reason for this is that mantra-based meditation tends to strengthen over time as the word or phrase becomes more familiar and more habituated. Do not confuse the term "habituated" with mind*less*ness. The focus of mantra work is always being aware in the present moment, as it is with all of the forms of practice we have already discussed; however, as the repetition of the mantra becomes ever more familiar, it can lead to surprisingly deep states of concentration of attention and temporal presence. In practice, the more familiar the mantra becomes, the more easily and quickly the attendant state of concentration can be conjured through its repetition, making the mantra an extremely accessible tool for consciousness training.

Seated Mantra Meditation

Mantra meditation can take many forms, including seated, standing, or lying down, as well as walking and even jogging. It can be done silently or spoken aloud as a repetitive chant. Below, I will give brief instructions for using a mantra for a seated concentration of attention exercise that can then be adapted to other physical postures or activities (again, see Mantra-Walking below). The instructions are nearly identical to those for the other exercises we have learned so far, but I will repeat them again for your convenience.

Mantra meditation, once established, is usually not performed as a guided meditation; so once you understand the instructions, you may continue by yourself, silently internalizing the syllables as your focal point of attention.

SEATED MANTRA MEDITATION

Instructions:

No cellphones or digital devices should be present in the room during this exercise, even vibration alerts are distracting. So, power the devices completely off and put them away, out of sight, before the session begins.

Sit on the floor on a cushion or mat and a meditation pillow to elevate your buttocks slightly above your knees (if you are sitting cross-legged). You can also sit on a chair with your feet on the ground in front of you, shoulder-width apart. Place your hands, palms up in your lap, right hand cradling left, with thumb tips lightly touching. Your hands and arms should be relaxed. You can also place your hands palms down on your knees. Once you've found your position, settle in and allow your awareness to turn inward.

While you can close your eyes, I recommend keeping them open and softly focused. If you are seated, you can let your eyelids droop slightly and pick a spot on the floor, between three and five feet in front of you, where you can focus without straining. Again, you want to have a soft focus so that while individual objects may be slightly blurred, you are still able to see the objects in your immediate field of vision.

Unless you otherwise cannot, due to blocked airways or the like, it is recommended that you keep your mouth closed during all meditation exercises and breath through your nose. While your mouth is closed, allow your tongue to rest, pressed gently against the front teeth. This will prevent excessive salivation and swallowing, which can be a distraction during an extended session.

Guidance Script:

Relax into position and turn your attention inward. You may want to take a few conscious breaths to center yourself.

When you are ready, begin to repeat the mantra of your choice silently to yourself.

Choose a slow to moderate rhythm that seems neither rushed nor sluggish to you. The tones of the mantra are best left fairly monotone, although you can choose to have the last syllable lilt up. The repetition should be in a continuous, deliberate "loop" with no discernible break between phrases.

> If it is helpful, you can begin the session by chanting the phrase out loud a few times to establish it in your head before fully internalizing it for your session. Speak each syllable distinctly and completely but without long pauses between syllables, so that the phrase flows smoothly and rhythmically in an effortless drone.
>
> As you repeat the mantra over and over, silently to yourself, make sure to remain present and attentive to each syllable as it repeats. The purpose of the exercise is identical to the breathing, body scan, and walking exercises in that attention to the object, in this case your mantra, is to remain steady and focused.
>
> When your mind wanders, gently and without judgment, bring it back to the next syllable of the mantra, or start again from the beginning if you have lost your place.
>
> Use a timer or session leader to track the time of the session so that you do not need to be concerned with checking the time or deciding when the session is over. If you pre-select the session length, this will eliminate the need to check the time, which is an unnecessary distraction.
>
> When the timer or the session leader indicates the session is over, gently let the mantra fade from your mind. You may want to take a few measured, conscious breaths as your attention broadens to include your surroundings and activities in the room.

Now that you have had some experience with a simple mantra meditation exercise, we will extend its use into other forms of movement and exercise.

The Mantra Workout

The first instruction for mantra-exercise (or any other kind of conscious fitness routine) is to eliminate all forms of digital entertainment and distraction during the exercise session and concentrate fully and intently on the activity at hand (this will also improve the quality and effectiveness of your workouts giving you maximum benefit). Even if you are doing weightlifting or some other kind of intensive workout that is not conducive to adding a meditative element, the time that you spend consciously focused on your activity, and not on media multi-tasking, is a period out of your day that discourages instead of encourages distraction and is, thus, of some value simply for that reason.

Below are the instructions for a basic mantra-exercise practice based on walking in an outside environment. The instructions can be adapted to all manner of sustained, repetitive aerobic exercise activities.

It is very difficult to conjure the appropriate amount of concentrative attention in group exercise activities except perhaps a group walk or run where participants are all utilizing the practice simultaneously.

The practitioner should always remain cognizant of any potential safety concerns and discontinue any concentrated meditative focus if it will in any way compromise the safety of an activity. This advice is particularly important if you choose to utilize exercise equipment or are in an environment that requires diligent attention to your surroundings, such as busy city streets or a weightlifting gym.

If you use an app or other device to track or monitor your exercise session, set it up before the session begins. With the exception of necessary heart rate monitoring, *plan on not interacting with any data until after the workout is complete.*

Do not use headphones or any other kind of auditory content input. Mantra-exercise is an attentional training exercise and, with the exception of the above-mentioned non-invasive data capture programs, all device interaction should be eliminated during the activity. Use this session as conscious device-free time during your day. Unless absolutely necessary, do not answer phones or texts during the session. If at all possible, it is recommended to leave all devices off, without the vibrate feature enabled, as any kind of device input during a meditation session, active or passive, is an unnecessary distraction.

MANTRA-WALKING/JOGGING EXERCISE

Instructions:

If you are walking or jogging outside, it is recommended to utilize a closed walking path where available. Your route should be familiar and safe, without undue hazards (such as heavily trafficked intersections). A well-defined walking path through a natural environment is ideal.

If you are mantra-exercising with others, it is best to agree in advance to forgo all conversation until the activity is over.

Do whatever necessary warm-up activities you require. You may take a couple of silent moments to center yourself, turn your attention inward, and become aware of your breath.

Begin your walking or jogging as you normally would. The pace of your exercise should be normal, not slowed or adapted as in walking meditation from the earlier chapter. For this version of mantra-exercise, use the mantra that you have selected for yourself. The focus of attention will primarily be on the repetition of the mantra and not on the physical sensations of the activity (such as in walking meditation).

Begin to recite your mantra in time with your steps. Depending on the mantra that you use, you might consider timing it so that it repeats every eight steps (or four steps, whatever is convenient), if you are using a single word or syllable, it might fit with every two steps. You might say the mantra out loud for the first several cycles to establish the rhythm pattern before internalizing the mantra and continuing with your normal exercise routine. Once you internalize the repetition of the mantra in rhythm with the activity,

> you might consider vocalizing the final syllable (if you are using a multi-syllable phrase) of each sequence, or on every eighth step if using a single word or syllable. Keeping the final syllable on every eighth step audible will help focus your attention on the mantra and make it easier to avoid losing track of the mantra altogether.
>
> During all mantra-exercise focus your attention on the mantra while remaining aware of your surroundings and environment, particularly as it relates to safety issues. As with any concentrative meditation practice, when you find that your mind has wandered from the object of attention (in this case the mantra), gently but firmly return the attention to the mantra and start again from the beginning.
>
> Continue the mantra repetition until the exercise period is finished.

Mantra-exercise can be a very effective way to combine multiple elements of a CMT program (discussed in more detail in the final chapter), including concentration practice, fitness training, and conscious "unplugging" moments throughout the day.

References

Bormann, J.E. (2010). Mantram repetition: A "portable contemplative practice" for modern times. In T.G. Plante (Ed.), *Contemplative practices in action: Spirituality, meditation, and health* (pp. 78–99). Santa Barbara: Praeger.

Cotman, C.W., & Berchtold, N.C. (2002). Exercise: A behavioral intervention to enhance brain health and plasticity. *Trends in Neurosciences*, *25*(6), 295–301. doi:10.1016/S0166-2236(02)02143-4

Cox, E.P., O'Dwyer, N., Cook, R., Vetter, M., Cheng, H.L., Rooney, K., & O'Connor, H. (2016). Relationship between physical activity and cognitive function in apparently healthy young to middle-aged adults: A systematic review. *Journal of Science and Medicine in Sport*, *19*(8), 616–628. doi:10.1016/j.jsams.2015.09.00doi:3

Daley, A.J. (2002). Exercise therapy and mental health in clinical populations: Is exercise therapy a worthwhile intervention? *Advances in Psychiatric Treatment*, *8*(4), 262–270. doi:10.1192/apt.8.4.doi:262

Donnelly, J.E., Blair, S.N., Jakicic, J., Manore, M., Rankin, J.W., & Smith, B. (2009). Appropriate physical activity intervention strategies for weight loss and prevention of weight regain for adults. *Med Sci Sports Exerc.*, *41*(2), 459–471.

Edwards, M.K., & Loprinzi, P.D. (2018). Affective responses to acute bouts of aerobic exercise, mindfulness meditation, and combinations of exercise and meditation: A randomized controlled intervention. *Psychological Reports*. doi:10.1177/0033294118755099

Erickson, K.I., Raji, C.A., Lopez, O.L., Becker, J.T., Rosano, C., Newman, A.B., … Kuller, L.H. (2010). Physical activity predicts gray matter volume in late adulthood. *The Cardiovascular Health Study*, *75*(16), 1415–1422. doi:10.1212/WNL.0b013e3181f88359

Erickson, K.I., Voss, M.W., Prakash, R.S., Basak, C., Szabo, A., Chaddock, L., … Kramer, A.F. (2011). Exercise training increases size of hippocampus and improves memory. *Proceedings of the National Academy of Sciences, 108*(7), 3017–3022. doi:10.1073/pnas.1015950108

Fabel, K., & Kempermann, G. (2008). Physical activity and the regulation of neurogenesis in the adult and aging brain. *NeuroMolecular Medicine, 10*(2), 59–66. doi:10.1007/s12017-008-8031-4

Fox, K.R. (1999). The influence of physical activity on mental well-being. *Public Health Nutrition, 2*(3a), 411–418. doi:10.1017/S1368980099000567

Gerber, M., Holsboer-Trachsler, E., Pühse, U., & Brand, S. (2016). Exercise is medicine for patients with major depressive disorders: But only if the "pill" is taken! *Neuropsychiatric Disease and Treatment, 12,* 1977–1981. doi:10.2147/NDT.S110656

Goldberg, P. (2010). *American Veda: From Emerson and the Beatles to yoga and meditation: How Indian spirituality changed the West* (first edition). New York: Harmony Books.

Goleman, D. (1988). *The meditative mind: The varieties of meditative experience* (first edition). Los Angeles and New York: J.P. Tarcher.

Hamilton, N.A., Nelson, C.A., Stevens, N., & Kitzman, H. (2007). Sleep and psychological well-being. *Social Indicators Research, 82*(1), 147–163. doi:10.1007/s11205-006-9030-1

Jacka, F.N., Cherbuin, N., Anstey, K.J., Sachdev, P., & Butterworth, P. (2015). Western diet is associated with a smaller hippocampus: A longitudinal investigation. *BMC Medicine, 13,* 215. doi:10.1186/s12916-015-0461-x

Kalak, N., Lemola, S., Brand, S., Holsboer-Trachsler, E., & Grob, A. (2014). Sleep duration and subjective psychological well-being in adolescence: A longitudinal study in Switzerland and Norway. *Neuropsychiatric Disease and Treatment, 10,* 1199–1207. doi:10.2147/NDT.S62533

Kelly, P., Williamson, C., Niven, A.G., Hunter, R., Mutrie, N., & Richards, J. (2018). Walking on sunshine: Scoping review of the evidence for walking and mental health. *British Journal of Sports Medicine, 52*(12), 800–806. doi:10.1136/bjsports-2017-098827

Lai, J.S., Hiles, S., Bisquera, A., Hure, A.J., McEvoy, M., & Attia, J. (2014). A systematic review and meta-analysis of dietary patterns and depression in community-dwelling adults. *The American Journal of Clinical Nutrition, 99*(1), 181–197. doi:10.3945/ajcn.113.069880

Mason, P. (1994). *The Maharishi: The biography of the man who gave transcendental meditation to the world.* Shaftesbury and Rockport: Element.

O'Neil, A., Berk, M., Itsiopoulos, C., Castle, D., Opie, R., Pizzinga, J., … Jacka, F.N. (2013). A randomised, controlled trial of a dietary intervention for adults with major depression (the "SMILES" trial): Study protocol. *BMC Psychiatry, 13,* 114–114. doi:10.1186/1471-244X-13-114

O'Neil, A., Quirk, S.E., Housden, S., Brennan, S.L., Williams, L.J., Pasco, J.A., … Jacka, F.N. (2014). Relationship between diet and mental health in children and adolescents: A systematic review. *American Journal of Public Health, 104*(10), e31–e42. doi:10.2105/AJPH.2014.302110

Otto, M.W., & Smits, J.A.J. (2011). *Exercise for mood and anxiety: Proven strategies for overcoming depression and enhancing well-being.* New York: Oxford University Press.

Pontifex, M.B., Raine, L.B., Johnson, C.R., Chaddock, L., Voss, M.W., Cohen, N.J., … Hillman, C.H. (2011). Cardiorespiratory fitness and the flexible modulation of cognitive control in preadolescent children. *Journal of Cognitive Neuroscience, 23*(6), 1332–1345. doi:10.1162/jocn.2010.21528

Sarris, J., Logan, A.C., Akbaraly, T., Amminger, P., Balanzá Martínez, V., Freeman, M., ... Jacka, F. (2015). Nutritional medicine as mainstream in psychiatry. *The Lancet Psychiatry*, *2*(3), 271–274.

Smits, A.J., Berry, A.C., Rosenfield, D., Powers, M.B., Behar, E., & Otto, M.W. (2008). Reducing anxiety sensitivity with exercise. *Depression and Anxiety*, *25*(8), 689–699. doi:10.1002/da.20411

Themanson, J.R., Pontifex, M.B., & Hillman, C.H. (2008). Fitness and action monitoring: Evidence for improved cognitive flexibility in young adults. *Neuroscience*, *157* (2), 319–328. doi:10.1016/j.neuroscience.2008.09.014

Utterback, N. (2017, May 5). Neil Utterback interview by K. Page.

Walsh, R. (2011). Lifestyle and mental health. *American Psychologist*, *66*(7), 579–592. doi:10.1037/a0021769

6

APPS, GADGETS, AND MINDFUL TECHNOLOGY USE

In recent years there has been an explosion of new apps and gadgets that purport to teach or support a meditation program of one sort or another. The general categories of available technology includes: mobile applications with various forms of content such as guided meditations, tracking programs, and social communities; "brainwave entrainment" equipment, which can include colored and/or white diode light glasses and the ability to generate Ganzfeld fields as well as audio binaural beats; individual EEG monitors that provide biofeedback data about what is going on inside the brain during meditation; and float tank sensory deprivation systems, which fall into a different category than the electronic devices.

In terms of available apps (and there will undoubtedly be more by the time this book is released), the majority provide meditation content on a premium subscription basis. This usually means that you download some version of the app onto your mobile device for free, and then, in order to be able to more fully utilize the features, track your progress, or acquire premium content, you sign up to pay a monthly subscription fee. The content that these apps provide varies from multiple guided meditations in both audio and video form factors; advice from teachers, usually consisting of canned, predetermined sets of generic instruction; various practical functions, such as meditation timers and alarms; social engagement with other users of the app; and encouragement or reward systems for keeping you motivated. In almost all cases, these apps were designed based on a social media platform of interaction and reward. The actual design of the digital platform is intended to keep you engaged *with the platform itself*. In almost all cases the value of these apps is represented as the input or interactivity that they offer. Even the simplest of meditation timer apps require you to keep your mobile device near you during the session, something *strongly discouraged* for serious meditation work, which can lead to the types of digital distraction discussed earlier. Alternatively, I recommend a mechanical egg timer, battery or wind-up powered, that does not tick or click, or a meditation timer that uses a traditional chime to indicate the end of a session. In group settings a time-keeper or leader can be responsible for tracking session times, allowing the individual participants to focus wholly on their individual meditation work.

From the perspective of a serious CMT program, nearly all of these apps need to be at least partially criticized and perhaps should be avoided altogether. On the one hand, they can act as a good portal for the inexperienced beginner who is curious about meditation training and perhaps needs some encouragement to begin. In that respect, these types of technology programs can be a useful entry point and even helpful. To the extent that they are included in any ongoing program, individual or group, I generally recommend that they be used like the scripted guided meditation examples provided in earlier chapters and discontinued as soon as the practitioners have gained a basic proficiency in the forms and learned to guide themselves. It appears that the vast majority of these apps are designed to *keep users using the app* and not concentrating intensely on their inner experiences or the arising of consciousness itself (the basic point of meditation training).

Another variation on the meditation app is the virtual reality meditation environment. Several programs are available on virtual reality platforms that offer multiple "meditation environments." These environments are often stunning, immersive landscapes such as mountain meadows, shoreline vistas, moonscapes, and other exotic virtual environments, often accentuated by accompanying soundtracks or guided versions of meditations. As with the apps discussed above, one must ask, however, what is the ultimate value of a visually striking (and attention-grabbing) virtual environment to the actual business of turning the attention inward and focusing on a single point of attention or paying intense attention to all experience as it arises? Once again, for the rank beginner, such programs may add some novelty to the activity as a starting point or a way to generate initial interest (by adding superfluous distracting elements) but might best be abandoned once the meditator begins to develop rudimentary skills controlling and deploying their attention function.

Muse

Muse is a $299 biofeedback device that measures brainwave activity through a fitted plastic headband embedded with seven electroencephalography (EEG) sensors that monitor your brain and transmit that data, using Bluetooth radio waves, to an app on your smartphone. The app then gives you feedback using soundscapes and imagery on your phone to help you target and identify "states of relaxation." The theory is that wearing the device while meditating can help "guide" you toward deeper, more relaxing meditative states.

In practice, the Muse headset is simple to use and the app has an orientation session that helps you calibrate the device to your body each time it runs. Muse offers a series of guided meditations, some of which are led by well-known personalities like Deepak Chopra, and a series of "soundscapes" that adapt to the data your brainwaves provide.

For example, Muse has an ocean-soundscape that starts with the sound of waves crashing on a beach. Depending on how agitated your brainwaves are, the waves sounds will be relatively loud and crashing like the sound of an approaching storm. But as you sit in silence, ostensibly trying to meditate to calm your brainwaves, the sounds of the waves on the shore become more calm and sedate. When you reach a certain level of brainwave sedation, birds begin to tweet along the shore, indicating that you have "attained a meditative state." The more birds you can get to chirp by deepening your calm, the better.

Like the other apps we have discussed, there is a subscription "premium" version of the app that unlocks additional guided meditations, soundscapes, and tracking functions so that you can build a progressive program of meditation training based on your own needs. And, like the other apps described, this can be a fun and entertaining way to otherwise start a regular meditation practice. However, once again, for those that take the work seriously and extend their practice over time, the sound games and guided meditations ultimately become a distraction to the deeper purpose of building a mindfulness practice.

Binaural Beats and Brainwave Entrainment Technology

Another type of gadget that purports to effect human consciousness is the so-called "brain/mind machine" or simply "mind machine." These devices usually consist of a digital player that operates a pair of stereo headphones and a set of goggles the user wears over closed eyes during the session. The session generally consists of a series of tones and sounds that "drive the brain waves" toward certain frequencies, while a set of light-emitting diodes attached inside the goggles flashes in various sequences directly in front of the user's closed eyes, creating a light show that is synchronized to the sound patterns (Huang & Charyton, 2008; Mikicin & Kowalczyk, 2015; Siever, 2012). The problem with such devices is that the science supporting their efficacy as either therapeutic interventions or trait-enhancing practices tends to be weak and far less plentiful than equivalent research on meditation and mindfulness. Additionally, even within what literature exists, there is little evidence suggesting that there is any actual correlated value in getting your brainwaves to concentrate in a particular frequency using external stimulation (Chaieb, Wilpert, Reber, & Fell, 2015; Dayalan, Subramanian, & Elango, 2010; Lavallee, Koren, & Persinger, 2011; Ossebaard, 2000). Yes, serious, intentional meditation practice can create effects in the brain that may alter brain wave frequencies, among other factors (Brefczynski-Lewis, Lutz, Schaefer, Levinson, & Davidson, 2007; Cahn & Polich, 2006; Chiesa, Calati, & Serretti, 2011; Fox et al., 2014; Tang, Holzel, & Posner, 2015); however, I have not been convinced by the manufacturers of these devices that entraining these brainwave states through audio tones and a light show is at all similar or equivalent to long-term brain changes created by meditative practice.

A representative example of the claims made by some of the manufacturers and distributors of these types of machines might include:

> Users of mind machines take advantage of rhythmic light and sound stimulation that has a powerful effect on mood and emotions. This stimulation can reduce stress, energize thinking, enhance creativity, help promote deep sleep, and assist in achieving calm and meditative states of mind ... Achieve deep relaxation and concentration at the touch of a button ... After a little practice, you can experience in minutes what used to take years of meditative practice to attain.

While I have noted a number of research studies above, I believe the evidence comes up far short of supporting such extravagant claims.

So, ultimately, the following discussion is meant as informational rather than prescriptive and the same caveats expressed for the apps and gadgets above apply: while such devices may represent and entertaining or motivating way to help in beginning the process of mindfulness training, they should be looked at as entry-level activities and left behind as soon as a more serious disciplined practice can be established. Further, both the audio and visual content of these devices directly contradict and act as a distraction from nearly all of the meditative practices already introduced in this book, with the possible exception of bare attention open monitoring.

In a typical mind machine session, the user will lay down in a comfortable position and don the earphones and diode-embedded goggles. Once the session begins and the diodes start to flicker, the user keeps their eyes closed as the flashing lights create their visual effects through the closed eyelids. Most such devices contain a variety of pre-programmed content (often with suggestive titles like "deep relaxation" or "cosmic consciousness" or "quick energy burst," suggesting to the user what type of stimulation they might expect from a particular session) that lasts between ten and 60 minutes. The session's audio content may be a combination of tones and sounds, often offset to slightly different frequencies in each ear, creating what is called a binaural beat (Chaieb et al., 2015; Lavallee et al., 2011; Yamsa-ard & Wongsawat, 2014). The light-emitting diodes (LEDs) embedded in the goggles, which may emit pure white light or a combination of various colors, can flash in all manner of combinations, creating a visually dazzling "lightshow" before the user's closed eyes. Often kaleidoscopic patterns will emerge in the user's visual field. The diodes can also create an even static light field, called a Ganzfeld effect (Wackermann, Pütz, & Allefeld, 2008) that can lead to low-level visual hallucinations (generally patterns of light behind the eyelids). The theory is that brainwave states (as evaluated by EEG equipment) can be coaxed or "entrained" by the sounds and light patterns, to replicate the same kinds of brain states as found in meditation practitioners, etc. Once again, the evidence is dubious, but the sessions can most assuredly be pleasant and entertaining, even relaxing. Individual discernment is encouraged, however, in evaluating whether these types of machines are worth the expense, which can reach several hundreds of dollars.

Flotation Therapy and Sensory Deprivation

Laboratory experiments on the effects of sensory deprivation began in the early 1950s at McGill University in Montreal, Canada. Scientists became interested in what happened to people's internal experiences and behavior when certain inputs from the senses were reduced or eliminated. These scientists developed experiments that involved such factors as total darkness, total silence, social and physical isolation, limiting the kinds and variability of stimulation, and physical confinement and restrictions of movement. They quickly discovered that when the senses were severely limited, consciousness (awareness) tended to focus on, and in some cases amplify, internal experiences (which included both kinesthetic and thought realms). Experimental subjects, isolated in enclosed tanks of body-temperature saltwater (so they would float effortlessly), without light or sound stimulation, often began to experience audio and visual hallucinations as well as altered states of mental consciousness.

Many of the early experimental subjects found their experiences uncomfortable and even disturbing, sometimes quitting the experiment before it was complete (Zubek, 1969, p. 3). Some of the McGill experiments involved monotonous stimulation rather than sensory deprivation, including such practices as restraining arms and legs, blindfolding, diffuse light, and white noise. Along with their experimenter's expectations, many of the subjects indeed did experience anxiety (Hutchison, 2003, p. 30). But in the mid-1950s a medical doctor named John C. Lilly, in collaboration with another doctor/researcher, Jay T. Shurley, developed a water-tank system for reducing sensory inputs, specifically including: the presence of other people (social isolation), light, sound, the effects of gravity (the subject was floating in a neutral-temperature water medium), and temperature (Hutchison, 2003; Lilly, 1977). The first tank design was constructed by modifying a sound and light-proof chamber that included a water tank that had been used to study the metabolisms of swimmers during World War II. The test subject was suspended upright in the tank of 93.5 degree water and fitted with a molded rubber helmet attached to a breathing hose (Hutchison, 2003, p. 28). But, by the 1970s, the original designs had been altered to have the floating subject lay down in a pool of heated saltwater, which allowed the subject to float on the surface of even small volumes of water, and several companies began building commercial versions of these floatation tanks.

In 1978, a popular novel entitled *Altered States* (Chayefsky, 1978) was released, followed by a film of the same name in 1980. This helped to spur a small cottage-industry of commercial floatation therapy centers where participants could pay a fee to partake in the flotation tank experience in one-hour increments (Hutchison, 2003, pp. 9–10). However, with cultural shifts in the 1980s and a backlash aimed at the excesses of movements like humanistic psychology and the human potential movement (Grogan, 2013), these flotation centers mostly declined and research into the area faded away. In response to those criticisms, however, flotation tank therapy and the use of such devices for their psychological and stress reduction effects have recently re-emerged under the general classification of restricted environmental stimulation therapy (REST) and commercial centers that provide the flotation tank experience are once again widely available in many metropolitan areas.

While many of the criticisms of the research on sensory deprivation remain valid (small subject pools, not enough controls, experimenter bias, etc.), the psychological effects are fairly well documented (van Dierendonck & Te Nijenhuis, 2005). Contemporary claims about the benefits of flotation therapy made by floatation centers include: improved overall mental and physical well-being; relief from back pain; recovery from fatigue; stress reduction; improved creative capacities; accelerated injury recovery and injury reduction; enhanced sports training; accelerated learning; and emulating the benefits of meditation (supposedly without the necessity of disciplined practice such as we are proposing in this book). While addressing these broad claims in detail is beyond the scope of this book, the stress reduction claim is of some interest to us. As mentioned in earlier chapters, stress is a major complaint of college-aged students and emerging adults. To the degree that flotation therapy is an aid in stress reduction, it should be listed as one alternative resource (where available). More importantly, perhaps, is the idea of using flotation therapy sessions as an adjunct to meditative training. It is worth noting that this technology is one of the only ones described in this chapter that actually supports the act of silent, introspective meditation training, whereas the other technologies all seem to add distraction to the process that eventually must be withdrawn (including: flashing lights, soundscapes, social media interactions, etc.).

Flotation therapy sessions, where available and economically feasible, can be used as a type of "mini-retreat," where the meditator uses the silence and solitude of the float session to engage in intensified sessions of either the body-scan or mindfulness meditation sequences introduced earlier, as an example.

In summary, the apps, gadgets, and technologies we have reviewed all have some potential to be helpful in either initially establishing a consciousness training practice or as adjuncts to an existing practice, however, as with the guided versions of the meditations themselves, these external devices are no substitute for developing a disciplined and sustained practice of directing the attention inwardly (and silently) in the traditional types of meditation exercises we have proposed.

References

Brefczynski-Lewis, J.A., Lutz, A., Schaefer, H.S., Levinson, D.B., & Davidson, R.J. (2007). Neural correlates of attentional expertise in long-term meditation practitioners. *Proceedings of the National Academy of Sciences, 104*(27), 11483–11488. doi:10.1073/pnas.0606552104

Cahn, B.R., & Polich, J. (2006). Meditation states and traits: EEG, ERP, and neuroimaging studies. *Psychological Bulletin, 132*(2), 180–211.

Chaieb, L., Wilpert, E.C., Reber, T.P., & Fell, J. (2015). Auditory beat stimulation and its effects on cognition and mood states. *Frontiers in Psychiatry, 6*, 70. doi:10.3389/fpsyt.2015.00070

Chayefsky, P. (1978). *Altered states: A novel* (first edition). New York: Harper & Row.

Chiesa, A., Calati, R., & Serretti, A. (2011). Does mindfulness training improve cognitive abilities? A systematic review of neuropsychological findings. *Clinical Psychology Review, 31*(3), 449–464. doi:10.1016/j.cpr.2010.11.003

Dayalan, H., Subramanian, S., & Elango, T. (2010). Psychological well-being in medical students during exam stress-influence of short-term practice of mind sound technology. *Indian J Med Sci, 64*(11), 501–507. doi:10.4103/0019-5359.102122

Fox, K.C.R., Nijeboer, S., Dixon, M.L., Floman, J.L., Ellamil, M., Rumak, S.P., ... Christoff, K. (2014). Is meditation associated with altered brain structure? A systematic review and meta-analysis of morphometric neuroimaging in meditation practitioners. *Neuroscience & Biobehavioral Reviews, 43*, 48–73. doi:10.1016/j.neubiorev.2014.03.016

Grogan, J. (2013). *Encountering America: Humanistic psychology, sixties culture, & the shaping of the modern self* (first edition). New York: Harper Perennial.

Huang, T.L., & Charyton, C. (2008). A comprehensive review of the psychological effects of brainwave entrainment. *Alternative Therapies in Health and Medicine, 14*(5), 38–50.

Hutchison, M. (2003). *The book of floating: Exploring the private sea*. Nevada City: Gateway Books and Tapes.

Lavallee, C.F., Koren, S.A., & Persinger, M.A. (2011). A quantitative electroencephalographic study of meditation and binaural beat entrainment. *Journal of Alternative and Complementary Medicine, 17*(4), 351–355. doi:10.1089/acm.2009.0691

Lilly, J.C. (1977). *The deep self: Profound relaxation and the tank isolation technique*. New York: Simon & Schuster.

Mikicin, M., & Kowalczyk, M. (2015). Audio-visual and autogenic relaxation alter amplitude of alpha EEG band, causing improvements in mental work performance in athletes. *Appl Psychophysiol Biofeedback, 40*(3), 219–227. doi:10.1007/s10484-015-9290-0

Ossebaard, H.C. (2000). Stress reduction by technology? An experimental study into the effects of brainmachines on burnout and state anxiety. *Appl Psychophysiol Biofeedback, 25*(2), 93–101.

Siever, D. (2012). Audio-visual entrainment: A novel way of boosting grades and socialization while reducing stress in the typical college student. *Biofeedback, 40*(3), 115–124.

Tang, Y.-Y., Holzel, B.K., & Posner, M.I. (2015). The neuroscience of mindfulness meditation. *Nat Rev Neurosci, 16*(4), 213–225. doi:10.1038/nrn3916

van Dierendonck, D., & Te Nijenhuis, J. (2005). Flotation restricted environmental stimulation therapy (REST) as a stress-management tool: A meta-analysis. *Psychology & Health, 20*(3), 405–412. doi:10.1080/08870440412331337093

Wackermann, J., Pütz, P., & Allefeld, C. (2008). Ganzfeld-induced hallucinatory experience, its phenomenology and cerebral electrophysiology. *Cortex, 44*(1), 1364–1378.

Yamsa-ard, T., & Wongsawat, Y. (2014). The relationship between EEG and binaural beat stimulation in meditation. Paper presented at the 7th 2014 Biomedical Engineering International Conference, November 26–28.

Zubek, J.P. (1969). *Sensory deprivation: Fifteen years of research*. New York: Appleton-Century-Crofts.

7

MINDFULNESS PROGRAMS AND INITIATIVES

As mentioned in Chapter 1, we will be using the term mindfulness in three distinct ways: mindfulness as a state of individual consciousness; mindfulness as a style of meditation training; and finally mindfulness as a cultural phenomenon or movement. So far, we have introduced several meditation practices that have included both FAM and OMM styles of meditation as well as formal and informal ways of engaging in mindfulness training (thus covering the first two usages). We have also looked at several issues that are prevalent in the emerging-adult age demographic and how college mindfulness training might help or improve complications in those areas. In this chapter, then, let us turn our attention to some of the programs and initiatives, particularly those tied to a university environment, that represent the institutionalization of the mindfulness movement (our third usage of the word).

Following are brief explorations of several types of contemporary programs that have evolved out of the mindfulness movement. We have already discussed the Koru program developed at Duke University and The Center for Mindfulness in Medicine, Health Care, and Society at UMass Medical School (the original home of the MBSR program), so the following explorations will add to the list of representative examples of just what is out there and available now. For the student who is interested in a career in the mindfulness industry, these brief outlines will provide a type of roadmap of emerging possibilities. In a book of this size, I have limited room, so look at the following profiles as representative only, examples of the kinds of programs being developed. I will provide a much longer list of contemporary programs and organizations in Appendix C at the end of this book which you can use as a more robust starting point for your own research and investigation into the field.

MindfulNYU

MindfulNYU is a meditation, mindfulness, and contemplative life initiative offered through the New York University Office of Student Affairs and administered by the Global Spiritual Life Center. MindfulNYU's mission is to promote wisdom, compassion, and well-being on the NYU campus—and beyond. In addition to curating resources that are available online, MindfulNYU hosts daily yoga classes, group meditations, large-scale events, and mindfulness workshops for students, faculty, and staff (New York University, 2018).

The senior director of the program is Yael Shy who is also author of the book, *What Now? Meditation for Your Twenties and Beyond* (2017). Shy began the program in 2009 as a result of her own experiences with meditation in college and her personal meditation practice. She started a meditation group for Jewish students through the Bronfman Center for Jewish Student Life at New York University but quickly broadened the scope to include students from any background who were interested in developing a meditation practice. As her efforts grew in popularity and expanded, New York University had just finished constructing a new building to house a number of its spiritual centers and provide a resource for student spiritual life in general. Shy became the co-director of the new building, helped develop its mandate and programs, and brought over the meditation groups she had sponsored into the new and larger facilities where the MindfulNYU program now has its permanent home.

> My background is in both Jewish meditation and I sat for many, many years with a Zen community, so I learned a lot of practices from within the Zen Buddhist world. We didn't really do any kind of Zen practices [when we first started], it's basically a secular program (the meditations we do) but we do reference Buddhist wisdom and Buddhist frameworks from time to time and we draw upon it quite a lot so that if students want to investigate it more deeply, they know where we're pulling this stuff from.
>
> (Shy, 2018)

From its humble beginnings as a single student-focused group, the MindfulNYU program has grown to include several ongoing practice groups which include instructor and student guided sessions of primarily secular meditation study. However, the many instructors and student-guided groups that are hosted come from various backgrounds that include Jewish, Buddhist, Insight (Theravadin), Vedic, and other traditional forms of meditation practice, as well as yoga training, and guest speakers that address a variety of topics of interest to both students and faculty.

> [As the program grew] we brought in a couple of other teachers, our main requirement was that they be very deeply rooted in a tradition or a practice

[of some kind], and that the students like them and they are able to work in a secular setting ... So basically what we have now is open meditation sessions; we have a Buddhist chaplain who leads the meditation session one night a week; and then we have a peer-led mindfulness group that meets one night a week. We have an advanced practice group that we started this year [2017], based on what people were asking us for. And then we have two small sub-communities, an LBGTQ meditation group and a people of color meditation group.

Each one is structured slightly differently depending on who teaches it, but for the most part, we start with maybe 15 to 20 minutes of a meditation with some guidance and some silence, then we usually have a discussion on some topic or a theme, like loneliness, or home, or friendship, or power, or something like that; and then will meditate [in silence] for the last 15 or 20 minutes. So that's our basic daily schedule. Then, we sometimes have guest speakers come. They are primarily from the Buddhist world but we've had Jewish meditation teachers come, we've had Christian and Muslim teachers come, we've had some teachers come that would be more from the Vedic tradition, and some others from the tantric, less Buddhism-connected, and then some people who are more secular teachers [not connected with any one tradition] ... So we have a little bit of a mix when it comes to the guest speakers.

(Shy, 2018)

In addition to their programmatic offerings, MindfulNYU offers a robust website with information and resources for students and faculty, including videos, audio (guided) meditations, a bibliography of books and formal research articles, and a list of apps, some of which are discounted by their publishers for currently enrolled New York University students.

Shy and her team also provide workshops and trainings for New York University's faculty and some of its remote campuses around the world.

We've done workshops in every single school of the university, that includes the education school, the law school, the medical school, the dental school, the nursing school, Tisch School of the Arts ... I would venture to say that between myself and my Assistant Director we have presented maybe 50 or 60 of these types of workshop? In 2014 we started a collaboration with the business school so we have a mindfulness in business program ... we also have a more in-depth collaboration with the school of social work where we share a minor in spiritual leadership, so those two programs we share a more in-depth relationship with ... And then NYU has many remote campuses around the world, and the reason the mindfulness program is run out of the Global Spiritual Life Center is that we visit these campuses every couple of years and do meditation instruction for staff, faculty, and students, everywhere from

Berlin, to Abu Dhabi, to Tel Aviv, to London. Those are some of the places we've been to teach these programs.

(Shy, 2018)

When asked why students seek out and join the various programs offered by MindfulNYU, Shy says:

> There really are a lot of common threads that come up, over and over again (and they really haven't changed that much since I was in college!) ... I would say, number one, is anxiety, and not just the kind of stress with school work, but real, overarching anxiety about issues like "what is my purpose here in the world?" "How am I supposed to balance all of the pressure that I'm hurting or struggling with?" Just a lot of fear and kind of a renegotiation of themselves in the world. Then, I would say, after that, there's loneliness and a desire for community, for connection; and that is both a desire for community within our meditation community but also I think they are really thinking about and concerned with their relationships, like romantic relationships, their friendships, and maybe lack of romantic relationships that they feel bad about ... We started doing mindful sex workshops over the last couple of years and they have been the most popular thing, not only for our entire meditation program but for our entire office that we've probably ever held ... The final theme that really comes up a lot, especially this year, is justice and social justice and the connection between the wider world and making change in the world, and these meditation practices.
>
> *(Shy, 2018)*

In her book, *What Now?* (2017), Shy engages in frank conversations about these types of issues and shares her personal experiences as both an anxious college student and a meditation practitioner. In the final chapter of this book I recommend including Shy's book as supplemental reading material for a curriculum outline in a for-credit course in both mindfulness training and the mindfulness movement/industry.

University of California—San Diego Center for Mindfulness

The University of California—San Diego (UCSD) Center for Mindfulness is a multi-faceted program of professional training, education, research, and outreach intended to further the practice and integration of mindfulness into all aspects of society. It offers a broad range of mindfulness-based programs and initiatives, on both individual and professional levels, including offerings for families and workplace environments. The center is a program of the UCSD Center for Integrative Medicine and UCSD School of Medicine's Department of Family Medicine and Public Health (Regents of the University of California, 2018b).

While they do offer some services to college students, the center's primary focus is on community outreach and teacher training in MBSR and related meditation protocols such as Mindfulness-Based Cognitive Therapy (MBCT). They offer classes in MBSR, mindful self-compassion, mindful eating, and mindfulness programs for kids, pre-teens, and teens. The center hosts silent retreats and has collaborated to create a mindfulness and peak performance training workshop called "mPEAK Training" that was developed in conjunction with the US National BMX Cycling Team, UCSD neuroscientists, and directors of the UCSD Center for Mindfulness (Regents of the University of California, 2018a).

One of the primary functions of the UCSD Center for Mindfulness is the training and professional certification of MBSR teachers (much like Jon Kabat-Zinn's Center for Mindfulness in Medicine, Health Care, and Society described in Chapter 3) through its Mindfulness-Based Professional Training Institute (MBPTI). The institute offers year-long teacher training in the MBSR protocol (as well as MBCT and Mindful Self-Compassion) and maintains a group of professional mentors that work directly with trainees to build experiential, hands-on teaching expertise before certifying graduates as a "Certified Teacher of MBSR" (Regents of the University of California, 2018c).

The MBSR training sequence involves two phases: Teacher Qualification and Teacher Certification. Teacher Qualification involves completing a number of prerequisites and a six-day teacher training retreat that is part silent meditation retreat and part didactic review of the basic MBSR protocol (see Chapter 3 for more detail on the protocol). Among the prerequisites required to attend this initial retreat are the satisfactory completion of the basic eight-week MBSR class, these are taught by previously certified teachers in many cities across the United States and the world, and also available as a home-study course that includes written materials, audio and video recordings (Meleo-Meyer & Santorelli, 2016); an established personal mindfulness meditation practice (formal sitting practice and informal practice); a mindful movement practice (yoga, t'ai chi, qigong, etc.); annual attendance at 5–7-day teacher-led silent meditation retreats in addition to the initial teacher training retreat; experience with teaching in a group setting and familiarity with group process (excluding teaching academic subjects). A formal application to enter the teacher training program is required that includes documentation of all of these prerequisites. In some cases where the applicant has a long-established practice or has already been a teacher in some other form of meditation training, some of these prerequisites can be waived or considered fulfilled by equivalence (as determined by the admission review committee).

Once the prerequisites have been met and the application to the program has been provisionally approved, the applicant is invited to complete the six-day MBSR Teacher Training Intensive and engage with a professional mentor who will supervise the teacher-in-training's activities for approximately the next year. Once the initial training retreat is completed, the teacher-in-training receives a

Provisional Certificate of Qualification that allows the trainee to offer MBSR classes to the public (under the supervision of their mentor).

In order to receive full certification as an MBSR teacher from the UCSD, MBPTI trainees must teach at least two eight-week MBSR courses with at least ten participants in each, and complete at least 22 hours of mentorship with an approved MBSR mentor during the teaching phase which may include review of teaching materials and audio or video recordings of the trainee's actual teaching (Regents of the University of California, 2018c).

Mindful USC

Mindful USC is a university-wide service provided through the Provost's Office with a mission of empowering the University of Southern California (USC) community to make positive change in the world by building a culture of mindfulness and compassion. The program was formally announced in 2014 and since has become very popular, serving approximately 1,000 students and faculty a year.

Mindful USC hosts a robust website that offers teaching videos, in-person class signup, and a free Mindful USC app available to university students, faculty, and members of the community at large. Classes in meditation practice include: Mindfulness Lab, Mindfulness Lab II, Mindful Writing, Mindfulness in Daily Life, and Mindful Self-Compassion. The program also offers silent retreats and guest speaker events throughout the year (University of Southern California, 2018).

The Mindful USC app includes such features as: push notifications of class, retreat and event announcements; the ability to sign up for Mindful USC classes; geolocation of closest on-campus practice groups; custom tailored meditations based on personal preference or mood; a meditation timer; ability to compete in USC mindfulness challenges; ability to connect with others and ask questions; progress tracking; and a library of guided meditations (provided by Mindful USC teachers).

As a university-based program directed primarily at students and faculty, Mindful USC is one of the most notable and well-funded efforts in the country right now. Outreach and proliferation efforts include offering program availability in every student orientation session throughout the USC system.

The Mindful USC program maintains strict standards for its meditation teachers. These standards are based on number of years and depth of personal practice and training as well as the study of mindfulness meditation practices and techniques. Teachers are also encouraged to embody the application of mindfulness in daily life. Mindful USC teachers are typically graduates of the Dedicated Practitioners Program (DPP) and/or Community Dharma Leaders Program (CDL) of Spirit Rock Meditation Center, MARC's teaching program, UCSD's teaching program or other training programs headed by well-known mindfulness guiding teachers. Mindful USC teachers are also required to continue as students themselves, and dedicate themselves to ongoing study (including yearly residential retreats) and to deepening continually their understanding and embodiment of mindfulness, much like the requirements for certified MBSR teachers through both the University of Massachusetts or USCD programs discussed earlier.

USC also offers a number of credit-bearing courses that include a mindfulness element or where mindfulness provides the underlying structure for the given course. Previous course titles include: *Mindful Aging: Spirituality, Gratitude, and Resilience; Leading with Mindfulness and Compassion; Music and Mindfulness: Strategy and Practice for an Ever Changing Field; Mastery in the Moment: The Science of Peak Performance; Mindfulness and the Creative Process*; and *Contemplative Neuroscience* (University of Southern California, 2018).

The Penn Program for Mindfulness

The Penn Program for Mindfulness is a program offered by Penn Medicine (the teaching hospital and medical research arm of the University of Pennsylvania). This program was founded by Dr. Michael Baime in 1992 and has trained more than 10,000 patients, doctors, and medical students in mindfulness techniques to help manage mood, stress, and quality-of-life issues. Baime started the program to offer stress reduction, primarily for cancer patients, but the program has since expanded to include almost all patient populations. Like the MBSR programs at the University of Massachusetts and UCSD detailed earlier, the Penn Program for Mindfulness also offers professional training for teachers of mindfulness as well as customized programs to support workplace mindfulness programs and community organizations that wish to apply mindfulness practices within their specific professional settings (The Center for Contemplative Mind in Society, 2018c).

The Penn Program's primary class offering is called Mindfulness-Based Stress Management and is very similar in scope and description to the MBSR protocol discussed earlier. In addition to this "foundation course," the program offers a variety of other classes and workshops, all open to the general public as well as University of Pennsylvania students and faculty. Some of these offerings include: *Introduction to Mindfulness* (two-hour workshop); *Showing-Up: Introduction to Mindful Writing* (two-hour workshop); *Stress-Out Kids: Mindfulness for Tweens and Teens* (four weeks); *Building a Mindful Writing Practice* (six weeks); *Open Sittings for People of Color* (ongoing, monthly). Following are brief descriptions of these course/workshop offerings.

The *Introduction to Mindfulness* two-hour workshops provide an overview of mindfulness and how it can potentially improve health, happiness, and quality of life while reducing stress. Potential benefits include:

- improved mood and energy;
- increased focus and mental clarity;
- improved management of difficult situations and emotions;

- enhanced communication;
- increased enjoyment and appreciation of life.

The mindfulness techniques introduced in this workshop help cultivate steadiness, health, and wholeness even during the most difficult moments. This training helps participants learn to connect with their inner resources in a simple and satisfying way (The Center for Contemplative Mind in Society, 2018c).

This brief two-hour workshop often serves as an introduction to and conduit for the eight-week Mindfulness-Based Stress Management course which many participants will later enroll in.

The *Showing-Up: Introduction to Mindful Writing* workshop introduces important concepts in applying mindfulness techniques to the writing process. Participants explore the potential benefits of applying mindfulness principals to their writing practice through a mix of meditation and writing exercises that focus attention in order to free the imagination (The Center for Contemplative Mind in Society, 2018c).

As with the Introduction to Mindfulness workshop above, this brief course serves as a conduit for the longer six-week version of the mindful writing workshop explained below.

The *Building a Mindful Writing Practice* is a six-week course that visits the concept of applying mindfulness practices to the ongoing creative writing process. Participants practice mindfulness meditation as well as specific exercises to unlock creativity and more fully explore the imagination while engaged in writing either fiction or non-fiction works.

Stress-Out Kids: Mindfulness for Tweens and Teens is a four-week program offered in partnership with the Children's Hospital of Philadelphia, that provides an age-appropriate introduction to mindfulness, including tools to help teens and tweens:

- decrease the effect of stress in their lives;
- increase focus and attention;
- help with emotional regulation;
- improve communication in relationships;
- increase a sense of wellness;
- be less reactive and more able to respond to the challenges of modern teen or tween life.

The goal of the course is to help this age group learn a variety of mindfulness techniques that include formal meditation practice (such as breath awareness, body-scan, and movement meditation), as well as information practices to use in daily life (The Center for Contemplative Mind in Society, 2018c).

In addition to these types of introductory courses, the Penn Program for Mindfulness also offers a variety of advanced mindfulness programs for individuals who have previously completed the eight-week Mindfulness-Based Stress

Management program either through Penn or another entity (such as MBSR training). Below are descriptions of the kinds of programs Penn typically offers:

- *Group practice sessions*—Sessions for practice and discussion *(live or via conference call)*.
- *Half-day retreats*—Three-hour silent guided mindfulness practice interspersed with talks and discussion.
- *Full-day retreats*—Topic-oriented workshops which include guided mindfulness practice, discussion, and application of specific mindfulness techniques.
- *Four-week programs*—A structured course to help participants to refresh their connection to and deepen understanding of mindfulness practice.
- *Eight-week programs*—Detailed exploration of mindfulness as related to a specific topic (e.g., anxiety or grief) or to the process of enhancing and refining personal practice.
- *Intensive retreats*—Four-and-a-half-day silent retreats that allow participants to abide in mindfulness and meditation, stillness and movement, and individual practice. These residential retreats are offered twice annually and contain longer periods of silence to support participants in fully immersing themselves in the experience of mindfulness.
- *Deepening Connections*—This year-long program is intended for participants who have established a regular meditation practice through either participation in the Mindfulness-Based Stress Management eight-week program or equivalent training. Significant experience with mindfulness as well as a willingness to go further on their path in a community is also required.
- *Individual Mentoring and Coaching*—One-on-one mindfulness-based mentoring and coaching intended to personalize and support a personal mindfulness practice and personal growth (The Center for Contemplative Mind in Society, 2018c).

Center for Contemplative Mind in Society

The Center for Contemplative Mind in Society (CMind) was formed in 1997 based on the mission to "transform higher education by supporting and encouraging the use of contemplative/introspective practices and perspectives to create active learning and research environments that look deeply into experience and meaning for all in service of a more just and compassionate society" (The Center for Contemplative Mind in Society, 2018c).

Since its founding, this organization has been dedicated to supporting transformation and engaged action for all through contemplative practices. In 2010, it re-focused its efforts on post-secondary education through its current initiatives of: supporting a network of scholars and academic professionals through the

Association for Contemplative Mind in Higher Education (ACMHE); hosting events including the Summer Session on Contemplative Pedagogy and the *ACMHE Annual Conference*; and creating resources and publications such as the *Journal of Contemplative Inquiry*, which was founded in 2014 by CMind as an online, peer-reviewed, interdisciplinary journal publishing articles, reflections, and book reviews to support the scholarly exchange of ideas regarding the understanding, development, and application of contemplative and introspective methods in all aspects of higher education (The Center for Contemplative Mind in Society, 2018c).

The ACMHE (CMind's current major initiative) is a multidisciplinary academic association with an international membership of educators, administrators, staff, students, researchers, and other professionals committed to the transformation of higher education through the recovery and development of the contemplative dimensions of teaching, learning, and knowing.

The ACMHE promotes the emergence of a broad culture of contemplation in the academy, connects a broad network of academic professionals with online resources, and stimulates scholarship and research concerning contemplative pedagogy, methodology, and epistemology within and across disciplines through initiatives and events including the annual ACMHE national conference (The Center for Contemplative Mind in Society, 2018b).

The ACMHE national conference is an annual interdisciplinary forum for all aspects of scholarship and research on contemplative methods in higher education, with a special focus on sharing how contemplative practices can support and sustain learning communities that foster a more just, peaceful, sustainable, and compassionate world (The Center for Contemplative Mind in Society, 2018a).

The Summer Session on Contemplative Pedagogy is an annual week-long intensive that prepares higher education professionals with resources to design and develop contemplative methods for their courses; create inclusive, inquiry-based learning environments; and incorporate contemplative awareness and practice within all aspects of higher education (The Center for Contemplative Mind in Society, 2018d).

CMind also hosts a robust website that provides many resources to the public and access to premium resources for ACMHE members which include free access to the *Journal of Contemplative Inquiry*, discounts for conference registrations, a membership directory, and an important Syllabus Archive that offers examples of syllabi from courses that incorporate contemplative approaches (The Center for Contemplative Mind in Society, 2018b).

The American Mindfulness Research Association

The American Mindfulness Research Association (AMRA) is another membership organization open to research professionals with either a doctoral or graduate degree, practice professionals (such as certified MBSR teachers, social workers or counselors, etc.), and students who are interested in the mindfulness movement. AMRA was founded in 2013 with a mission to support empirical and conceptual efforts to: (1) establish an evidence base for the process, practice, and construct of mindfulness; (2) promote best evidence-based standards for the use of mindfulness research and its applications; and (3) facilitate discovery and professional development through grant-giving. The AMRA serves as a professional resource to the sciences and humanities, practice communities, and the broader public on mindfulness from the perspective of contemplative practice (American Mindfulness Research Association, 2018).

The AMRA provides a comprehensive database of over 5,000 mindfulness references. Members have full access to download this database to support their own work and to keep pace with the rapid world of scientific publishing focused on evidence-based mindfulness research. The AMRA also provides for its members a scientific database of academic publication references on mindfulness from a contemplative psychology and practice perspective. The AMRA Library warehouses this compendium of references that can be downloaded for personal use with a reference management program such as Endnote. The AMRA sponsors several mindfulness events and conferences with affiliate organizations throughout the year that provide opportunities for AMRA members to network. Additionally, Research and Practice Professional Development grants are made available each year to early career professionals (American Mindfulness Research Association, 2018).

One of the more important benefits to AMRA membership is the *Mindfulness Research Monthly* publication that tracks recent publications and the release of new scientific research in the mindfulness field.

Mindful Schools

Mindful Schools is a 501(c)(3) non-profit organization that offers teacher training and other resources through a website aimed at K-12 educators and school environments. Founded in 2007 by a group of educators, the Mindful Schools program began in a single classroom at Emerson Elementary School in Oakland, CA. By 2010, it was serving more than 50 schools in the San Francisco Bay area. By 2012, Mindful Schools was launched as an online teacher training platform, and as of this writing, it claims to have trained over 25,000 educators, parents, and mental health professionals, in 100+ countries, cumulatively reaching over two million school-aged children worldwide. It currently has a staff and faculty of more than 30 professionals in the mindfulness, non-profit, and social justice fields (Mindful Schools, 2018).

Primarily through its website, Mindful Schools offers course packages (for a fee) to teachers and other professionals (including interested parents) in both developing a personal mindfulness practice (a prerequisite for the teacher training) and teaching a basic system of mindfulness to students in the K-12 classroom. In addition to its basic courses, Mindful Schools also offers a year-long teacher certification program that can be taken for continuing education or graduate credit (Mindful Schools, 2018).

The basic Mindful Schools training package includes two parts: *Mindfulness Fundamentals*, a six-week online course that includes the basics of mindfulness meditation through a series of videos, readings, reflections, and guided mindfulness practices intended to establish the educator's personal mindfulness practice (a prerequisite to the teacher training); and *Mindful Educator Essentials*, which is the basic online course aimed at classroom teachers, mental health professionals, social workers, and parents who want to integrate mindfulness into their work with youth using the research-based K-12 Mindful Schools Curriculum (Mindful Schools, 2018).

The *Mindfulness Fundamentals* course covers current scientific research on mindfulness and the brain, emotion regulation, and compassion. The course is facilitated by an experienced Guiding Teacher who directs the learning process by answering questions, providing ongoing feedback, and synthesizing emerging themes. The course content includes:

- basics of mindfulness meditation;
- how to work with thinking that arises while practicing mindfulness;
- techniques for meeting and navigating intense emotions;
- practices that cultivate positive states of mind like gratitude, kindness, joy, and compassion;
- the role mindfulness plays in communication and interaction;
- support for developing a daily sitting practice.

Other secular mindfulness training can be substituted as the prerequisite for moving on to the *Mindful Educator Essentials*, including MBSR or MBCT training sequences as provided by the University of Massachusetts and USCD programs (and others) mentioned earlier (Mindful Schools, 2018).

The *Mindful Educator Essentials* course is a six-week self-paced course that includes:

- Curriculum for All Levels
    - a   Pre-K to 2 Kindness Curriculum: 24 modules for ages 3–6, from Center for Healthy Minds
    - b   K to 5 Curriculum: 30 modules for ages 5–12
    - c   Middle & High School Curriculum: 25 modules for ages 12–17.
- Student workbooks.
- Manuals on facilitation, classroom management plus a Parent Manual and Classroom Manual.
- Summaries of neuroscience concepts.

- Program evaluation tools.
- Access to over 150 resources for teaching mindfulness to youth available from the Mindfulness Schools website.
- Resources to present to administrators, school, and agency staff.

The Mindful Teacher Year-Long Certification Program requires a minimum of 300 hours of training that includes evaluation of teaching skills by Mindful Schools authorized senior trainers. The program begins and ends with in-person, week-long residential retreats. In between retreats, participants engage in an intensive ten-month virtual training program that includes the following activities:

- *Online content*—Instructional videos, readings, and reflection assignments that track the course's key themes as they unfold over the ten months.
- *Live group calls*—Engaging discussions, lectures, guided sits, and Q&A formats via Zoom video calls. (Most live calls are recorded for later viewing.)
- *Cohort group*—Dedicated small groups with whom reflection assignments and practice teaching feedback is shared. Groups stay connected through online discussion and monthly, hour-long live video calls led by Guiding Teachers.
- *Daily sitting*—Participants are asked to maintain a personal mindfulness practice of at least 20 minutes per day.
- *Expert-led workshops and talks*—Engaging live talks and webinar-style workshops with faculty of contributing teachers who are leaders in the mindfulness and education movement.
- *Teaching lab*—Participants record and share video of themselves teaching a group of youth and receive feedback on their teaching from their Guiding Teacher and cohort group.
- *Additional learning experiences*—teacher office hours, reading groups, sitting groups, and regional meet-up groups (where possible).

The Mindful Teacher certification allows Mindful Schools Certified Mindfulness Instructors (CMIs) to:

- Use and teach the Mindful Schools curriculum to adapt mindfulness programs to the needs of specific school settings, classroom routines and content areas, as well as integrate mindfulness instruction into various types of learning activities.
- Teach adults the fundamental practices and principles of mindfulness by offering introductory or beginner-level mindfulness classes. Also to lead mindfulness practice with groups of teachers, administrators, parents, or other interested members of the school community or institution.
- Lead professional development efforts related to mindfulness practice, the field of mindfulness in education, the benefits of teaching mindfulness to youth, and the benefits of youth caregivers having a personal mindfulness practice.

- Support efforts to design a mindfulness program for school communities or similar institutions, and mentor teachers and administrators in their work to establish and develop a mindfulness program (Mindful Schools, 2018).

As you can see from the description, the Mindful Schools certification process is similar to the MBSR certification described earlier. However, it should be pointed out that one very consistent requirement of all of these teaching protocols (including College Mindfulness Training) is that *the teacher must have a personal experiential practice* of their own to effectively teach the practices. That hands-on, personal experience of mindfulness practice simply cannot be overlooked or circumvented, it is an essential element of the teaching process.

References

American Mindfulness Research Association. (2018). American Mindfulness Research Association Website. Retrieved from https://goamra.org/.

The Center for Contemplative Mind in Society (2018a). Annual ACMHE Conference Website. Retrieved from www.contemplativemind.org/programs/conferences.

The Center for Contemplative Mind in Society (2018b). The Association for Contemplative Mind in Higher Education Website. Retrieved from www.contemplativemind.org/programs/acmhe.

The Center for Contemplative Mind in Society (2018c). The Center for Contemplative Mind in Society (CMind) Website. Retrieved from www.contemplativemind.org/.

The Center for Contemplative Mind in Society (2018d). Summer Session on Contemplative Pedagogy Website. Retrieved from www.contemplativemind.org/programs/summer.

Meleo-Meyer, F., & Santorelli, S. (2016). *The MBSR home study course: An 8-week Training in mindfulness-based stress reduction—workbook edition*. Louisville: Sounds True Publishing.

Mindful Schools. (2018). Mindful Schools Website. Retrieved from www.mindfulschools.org/.

New York University. (2018). MindfulNYU Web Page. Retrieved from www.nyu.edu/students/communities-and-groups/student-diversity/spiritual-life/mindfulness.html.

Regents of the University of California (2018a). mPEAK Web Page. Retrieved from https://health.ucsd.edu/specialties/mindfulness/mpeak/Pages/default.aspx.

Regents of the University of California (2018b). UCSD Center for Mindfulness Website. Retrieved from https://health.ucsd.edu/specialties/mindfulness/Pages/default.aspx.

Regents of the University of California (2018c). UCSD Mindfulness-Based Professional Training Institute Website. Retrieved from http://mbpti.org/programs/mbsr/mbsr-teacher-certification/.

Shy, Y. (2017). *What now? Meditation for your twenties and beyond*. Berkeley: Parallax Press.

Shy, Y. (2018, December 21). Yael Shy interview by K. Page.

University of Southern California. (2018). Mindful USC Website. Retrieved from http://mindful.usc.edu/.

8

INDIVIDUAL CMT PRACTICE

College Mindfulness Training (CMT) is more than an explication of various types of meditation and an exploration of the field of mindfulness in general. The goal of CMT is to take both the information and the exercises introduced so far and use them as components of a personal ongoing mindfulness practice. Whether you have studied this material in a classroom setting or as an individual simply reading this book up to this point, ultimately you will want to take what you have learned and implement it. So, just what is a "CMT practice" and how is it different from the simple exercises that have been introduced so far?

A CMT Practice: Individual and Collective Approaches

Many people who are introduced to meditation of various forms through a class or workshop session will do the experiential work during the class or workshop but skip the homework sessions in between classes and cease meditating after the class or workshop is complete. That is a perfectly appropriate way to be introduced to meditation and mindfulness, but it is not a "practice" per se. *A mindfulness practice is an ongoing experiential activity that is intentional and sustained over time.* If you only do the various exercises during class and read the chapters of this text when assigned, you will gain very few of the actual benefits of a formal mindfulness practice. In order to reap the sustained benefits attributed by the research to mindfulness meditation practices, you will need to establish a regular practice that becomes a part of your ongoing daily routine, very much like exercise becomes a regular part of a fitness routine.

The physical exercise/fitness analogy can be a useful one as many college-aged students have had experience, though athletics programs in many cases, with fitness and conditioning training. Let's imagine that you are starting a new personal fitness program to lose weight and tone your muscles. Your goal is to lose ten pounds and to trim down your waist by a couple of inches. You might start by looking at your diet and adjusting what you eat. You would also want to start exercising regularly, say jogging two times a week and lifting weights three times a week. So, in this example so far, you have set a goal (to lose ten pounds and trim your waistline) and planned out how you will work toward your goal over time (a diet and exercise program). Now, if you stop here, having merely set a goal and made a plan, how much success do you think you could expect? The answer, of course, is none! You have not yet *done* any of the actual work required to implement your plan and achieve your goals. (That would be the equivalent of reading this book but never taking the time to do any of the exercises.) Returning to our example, what if you didn't change your diet at all and only jogged once a week for a month, keeping your old lifestyle and ignoring the gym altogether. Will you have reached your goals? Again, the answer is: no. In order to lose ten pounds and trim two inches off your waist, you would probably need to follow your entire plan (diet, jogging, and weights) for at least a couple of months before you could expect to see the kind of results you were hoping for. The same can be said about a CMT practice: an intention/goal, a plan for reaching that goal, and consistent work over time are all required to see the kinds of results generally promised by the research presented in the earlier chapters of this book.

For the remainder of this chapter, I will lay out in some detail an outline for an individual CMT practice based on the exercises already presented. In the next chapter, I will lay out the parameters for a college-level course that, when the sequence is completed, will leave the students with all of the basic skills and understandings necessary to continue with an individual CMT practice after the course has concluded. So, this chapter addresses the needs of the individual interested in establishing a personal practice, while the next chapter is addressed to the college instructor who wants to develop a for-credit college offering.

Goal and Intention Setting

In the 1960s, Edwin A. Locke began research into whether or not people's goals and intentions really played any significant role in their successes at job performance. He developed a theory around goal-setting and concluded that people were more motivated and had better task performance outcomes when their goals were *difficult and challenging* rather than easy and mundane. He also found that behavioral intentions tended to regulate the kinds of choices people made, and in some cases the types of risks they were willing to take, in order to achieve specific goals (Locke, 1968). In other words, *intention is related to commitment.*

In a more recent meta-analysis of the literature on motivation and goal-setting (Gollwitzer & Sheeran, 2006), researchers acknowledged the value of basic goal-setting, *à la* Locke, but then went further: "[They] proposed that successful goal achievement is facilitated by a second act of willing ... termed *implementation intentions*" (2006, emphasis added). Implementation intentions, in these researchers' view, are essentially if/then plans that are triggered by certain premeditated events set by the goal maker. In our example of the fitness program above, the goal would be the same (lose weight, tighten waistline), and the implementation intentions would be the specific ways the goal-maker plans to go about doing the necessary work under various anticipated circumstances to achieve the goal. For instance, if the work plan was to jog twice and lift weights three times a week, the goal-maker might set a contingency for if it were to rain on one of her jogging days: "If it rains on my jogging day, I will do an hour on the indoor treadmill instead." Having a set of implementation intentions in place helps the goal-maker identify opportunities and possible obstacles to the execution plan and this practice tends to keep a plan of action (one of the core components of a successful mindfulness practice) from becoming interrupted or derailed by circumstances much better than a simple positive attitude (Gollwitzer & Sheeran, 2006).

In very clear language, Gollwitzer and Sheeran (2006) state that "implementation intentions appear to be effective at enhancing the likelihood of goal achievement" (p. 70). So, it would appear that successful intention-setting is actually a two-step process: first setting an intention to accomplish a goal (such as engaging in an ongoing and sustained mindfulness practice); then setting specific intentions around when, where, and how you want to achieve those goals utilizing available and emerging resources.

In explaining why they thought implementation intentions seemed to be a better predictor of actual goal achievement, beyond merely having a general intention (positive attitude) to achieve a goal in the first place, Gollwitzer and Sheeran defined four general obstacles that often interfere with the goal achieving process: (1) failing to get started; (2) starting but getting derailed; (3) not calling a halt to goal striving that has become unproductive; and (4) overextending oneself. All of these situations tend to require self-regulatory behaviors to keep the goal seeker on track, particularly over time in the quest to accomplish difficult types of meta-goals (such as a mindfulness practice); and that was where the researchers felt that the planning required by implementation intentions was useful in the ultimate acquisition of the desired goal (Gollwitzer & Sheeran, 2006, pp. 82–86).

Basic Parameters of an Individual CMT Practice

The basic requirements (or tools) necessary to implement a CMT practice are minimal. In preparing to start CMT, you should have access to or acquire:

- A quiet space where you can sit (or lie down) as needed for up to 30 minutes without interruption.
- Appropriate padding for your comfort, pillows for sitting, perhaps a yoga pad and some rolled up blankets to support your head and knees when lying down.

- An egg timer or (non-ticking) alarm clock for timing your sessions (you should probably avoid using a cellphone for this purpose as even vibration alerts from a muted phone are distracting).
- Either a tape recorder for playback of guided meditations, or, in this case, a cellphone could be permitted as a playback device until you have memorized the instruction sets and no longer require the guidance.
- If you are using any apps or gadgets in the early stages of establishing a practice, you should have made those acquisitions and understand how to operate them before you start so that your full attention can be focused on the exercise and not the device delivering the content.

The point of preparing your space and equipment (if any) in advance is to limit any distractions during your actual practice sessions.

If you are using guided versions of the meditations to begin, it is easy if you are working in a group with others, simply select one group member to read the guidance scripts provided earlier in this book. If, however, you are working completely alone, you can either record your own versions from the scripts in the book or look on the Internet where you will find many comparable guided recordings available for free (they may not be word-for-word identical, but they can serve the purpose of teaching you the basic forms until you no longer need the external guidance). As stated in several places earlier, the guided versions of the meditation practices should be relinquished as soon as possible in favor of internalizing all directions.

Below, I will lay out a basic outline for establishing a CMT practice over a six-month time frame. This outline will assume 30 minutes of practice every day although five days a week is adequate for an effective CMT practice. Feel free to modify any of the parameters to fit your own particular circumstances. The important thing is to set a firm intention to establish and maintain a practice over time and to understand and commit to the activities required to execute on your plan (implementation intentions).

During the course of your initial CMT program you may well want to participate in one or more silent retreats as indicated below. There are numerous retreat centers around the country, often accessible in your local area, with many other options available if you are willing to travel. These centers will offer structured retreats based on various forms or styles of meditative practice. Mindfulness retreats (sometimes called Vipassanā) are very popular and widely available. As always when operating alone, make sure to do your research and only commit to reputable programs run by established centers with good records. You want to feel comfortable and supported in the retreat setting and having confidence in the teacher or retreat leader is very important for cultivating the proper state of mind to release yourself wholly to the experience. The Center for Mindfulness in Medicine, Health Care, and Society at the University of Massachusetts Medical School, founded by Jon Kabat-Zinn, maintains on its website a list of retreat center facilities that qualify under its MBSR teacher training program and that might be a useful resource for you (Center for Mindfulness, 2017).

You may also want to seek out a meditation group or formal meditation teacher for support in you CMT journey. A meditation teacher and/or group affiliation can be very helpful on a number of levels. First, if you have questions as your practice develops, a trained and experienced teacher is a valuable resource of knowledge and answers. Most meditation teachers have had extensive personal meditation experience and so have "been there before." Also, having a teacher or being part of a group can help motivate you to keep going with your practices even when the temptation to quit or slack off arises (which it inevitably does with almost everyone at some point during the first year). Additionally, silent meditation with a group tends to heighten the level of concentration and effectiveness of a meditation session, so that sitting with a group on a regular basis can actually speed the progress of your practice beyond what you might be able to accomplish all on your own. So, find a meditation teacher or community in your area and give it a try. If you like the environment and the individuals involved, stick with it. If not, move on to the next resource until you find a group and teacher that fit your individual needs. In most major cities today, you will have a number of choices and options available to you. You can certainly begin practice on your own, but it is very likely that at some point you will want to seek out a teacher or meditation group.

A Sample Individual CMT Program

The exercises in this book have been presented in a progressive order, starting with simple attentional training exercises that build to the more complex exercises that require more focus of attention. However, to this point, I have not suggested an actual structure and timeframe for a program based on these exercises. Below, I will offer just such an example. Again, this is only an example and can be modified to fit your own particular situation as needed. The primary goal is to establish a regular practice that can be maintained over time.

It is assumed that you have read this book up to this point before committing to a formal practice. If not, I recommend going back and reading all seven chapters which will give you the meditation forms, their purposes and backgrounds, and present a formal logic for the progression I outline below.

THE FIRST MONTH

Review Chapter 1 of this book, paying particular attention to the exercise instructions and rational.

Starting with the *Watch Exercise* and the *Mindful Eating Exercise #1* in Chapter 1 as a way of setting a benchmark for yourself. Both of these exercises will tell you something about your own attention span and ability to deploy that attention to specific objects. Initially, this willful direction of attention will be the major focus of our experiential work, the "muscle" we are trying to strengthen. Once we gain some control over this attention muscle, we will add exercises that use this newly strengthened muscle to more advantage.

In the first week of formal CMT practice, plan at least three (or preferably five) 30-minute practice sessions where you can inhabit your previously prepared space without interruption or distractions. If you can, try to plan these sessions for the same time each day as that may help you establish a regular habit and help you compare the experiences of individual sessions.

In the first week's sessions, you will be practicing the *Conscious Breathing Exercise* from Chapter 1. You can have someone read the instructions or can record your own voice reading the guidance instructions. By the end of this week, you should fully understand the instructions and be able to do a 30-minute session of Conscious Breathing on your own without external guidance. Usually, internally guided meditation sessions allow for deeper concentration on the object of meditation than the externally guided versions. However, feel free to use the guided narration as long as is necessary to become comfortable with the instructions and internalize them.

In the second week, move on to the *Traditional Body-Scan*, also found in Chapter 1. This exercise can be done in 30 or 40 minutes. Again, try and plan for between three and five sessions during this week, and either find a leader to read the narration aloud, or pre-record your own voice reading the directions. (If making your own recording, make sure to leave plenty of time to enact the instructions; do not rush.) Many people find that the body-scan, particularly initially, may put them to sleep. This is natural and also relaxing! However, if you find that you are falling asleep too often, you can try keeping your eyes open, but in a soft focus. Also, if you have been laying down, try sitting in a chair for the body scan. As before, with the Conscious Breathing exercise, by the end of a week, you should have the basic instructions memorized and be able to do the full body-scan using internalized self-guidance.

For week three, plan on a full five sessions (that is only two-and-a-half hours for the week, to put the commitment into perspective, which is far less time than you are probably spending on your college courses or even your physical workouts each week). Alternate the Conscious Breathing and the Traditional Body-Scan exercises, one Monday–Wednesday–Friday and the other Tuesday–Thursday. This will give you experience with two distinct types of meditation training, one based on movement and breath, the other based on stillness and awareness shifted to various parts of the body. The primary activity in both types of meditation exercise is the focusing of the attention on specific sensations that can be easily brought into consciousness by the will. This ability to direct attention will improve with practice, so don't be frustrated if your mind seems to wander a lot at first (this is very natural), and simply and gently return your attention to the focus of the exercise.

In week four, simply switch the exercises you did last week so that whichever one you did for three days, you now do for two; and whichever one you did for two days now goes to three days.

By the end of this first four-week cycle, you should be very comfortable doing either the Conscious Breathing and the Traditional Body-Scan exercises without external guidance and these exercises should be starting to feel familiar (and maybe even a little easier than when you first started). You will keep these very basic exercises in your repertoire and return to them often as core pillars of your CMT practice.

In this first month, you have learned to internalize the instructions of two basic FAM exercises. As I have mentioned before, at the beginning of a CMT program it is very likely that you will struggle with your own mind and thought streams. It definitely will take time to begin developing an ability to catch any distracting thoughts or sensations, acknowledge them in a non-judgmental way, and gently but firmly lead your attention back to the object of meditation. It may seem that the meditation practice is "making your thoughts race." However, this is normal and usually a function of simply becoming aware of how fragmented and active your thinking processes already are. When you first look inside at the activity of your own mind, it can be very surprising to find out how chaotic your thinking has been on a daily basis *without your being aware of it*. Expect for it to take a substantial amount of time and work before you begin to see noticeable improvement in your control over your attention and a general calming of mental "noise." Be assured that with practice you will first become better at staying focused and eventually the degree of fragmentation and fervor of your thoughts and emotions will begin to stabilize. That is why we start with FAM training in the first place, to gain at least a minimal amount of control over the attentional function before we advance into other forms with less structure.

THE SECOND MONTH

Review Chapter 2 of this book, paying particular attention to the exercise instructions and rationale.

Additionally, in month two, you can start to add in some what I call *mindfulness of technology*, as this will help with one of the most pernicious impediments to consciousness and attentional control in our postmodern times: technologically induced distractions and compulsive multi-tasking (discussed at length in both Chapter 2 and Chapter 4). Mindfulness of technology can take many forms, such as fully powering down your digital devices and putting them out of site for predetermined periods throughout the day; taking technology retreats, where you remain unplugged for one- or two-day periods while being mindful of any feelings of loss or addictive cravings; and during social/group events, consciously engaging in direct conversations with peers when appropriate instead of retreating into your cellphone or tablet as a type of social defense mechanism.

Some general goals could be: (1) to reduce the amount of time that digital technology is available and accessible throughout your day by two hours; (2) to not play a television "in the background" unless actively engaged in the programming; (3) to stop multi-tasking behaviors that encourage task-switching and chronic distraction, such as social media use while studying or using another type of media, and so forth. Much of the research we reviewed in Chapter 2 indicated that repeated and unconscious multi-tasking behavior was the activity most damaging to the ability to deploy and focus attention, and it is our goal to *improve* that ability. Therefore, to the degree that you can reduce such behavior and make it conscious (rather than unconscious) when you do engage in it, you are increasing self-awareness and training your consciousness while reducing the unwanted side effects of the behavior.

The primary meditation practice during month two will be *FAM on the Breath* (see Chapter 2 for the instructions and a guidance script). As in month one, your goal will be between three and five half-hour sessions during the week, generally around the same time of day if possible.

FAM on the Breath is usually performed in a seated position with eyes open but with a soft focus. This will generally tend to ameliorate any problems with falling asleep.

As with previous exercises, by approximately the end of week one, you should fully understand the instructions and leave off using audible guidance for an internally directed meditation experience. Also, in many ways, FAM on the Breath is a simpler exercise, merely requiring you to focus on the life-sustaining activity of breathing instead of multiple physical movements or a shifting array of body parts.

In week two, after having left off the external guidance, you can begin Counting or Labeling Breaths variation described at the end of Chapter 2. This will most likely make it easier for you to keep the attention on the breathing process, particularly at this early stage of your practice, and give you an "anchor" to bring your attention back to the breath when you inevitably become distracted. Continue the counting of the breaths for the rest of the sessions in month two. In most cases, you will stay with the counting of the breaths variation for several months until it is easier for you to aim and hold your attention on the breathing process without the counting.

If you have only been able to do three sitting sessions per week up to this point, do try to extend your weekly number of sessions to five by the time you reach week six of your practice. Thirty minutes per day, five days per week, is generally an optimal "dosage" of FAM-style meditation to begin to

> experience the benefits of a meditation practice as generally described in earlier chapters. So, do try to get up to five sessions per week if at all possible.

After two months of regular practice you have mastered the basic forms of three district types of FAM meditation and have begun to become more aware of your technology use. Congratulations! That is quite an accomplishment. You may be starting to notice some benefits from your practice such as an easier time focusing and maintain a focus of attention, a calmer, more grounded attitude in general, and a reduction in generalized stress. If, on the other hand, you feel you are still not seeing any tangible results, do not worry or become self-critical. Everyone responds to meditation training in their own unique way, so simply keep after it.

You may also have realized that the stream of thoughts that often distract your focus never really go away, they just become easier to manage. Many people have the mistaken idea that meditation practice is about stopping the flow of thoughts (which is actually impossible), but in reality, this kind of training is really more about repeatedly and gently returning the attention to the object of the session (breath, bodily sensations, etc.); it is this repeated marshalling of the attention that eventually shows results, not the suppression of consciousness.

THE THIRD MONTH

Review Chapter 3 of this book, paying particular attention to the exercise instructions and rationale.

In month three, as we did in month one, we will alternate exercises on even and odd days once the new exercise (Mindful Movement—Walking) has been learned.

So, month three begins with the *Mindful Movement—Walking* exercise introduced in Chapter 3. Use the guidance script, as you have before, in the first week or so to master the form and instructions and then continue the exercise with internal guidance only. After the first week (five sessions) begin to alternate sessions of Mindful Movement—Walking with sessions of FAM on the Breath for a total of at least five 30-minute sessions a week for the remainder of the month.

As a way to deepen your understanding of meditation practice, you are also invited to read some of the supplemental material provided in the reference lists at the end of each chapter and the partially annotated Appendix at the end of the book. These optional readings will give you multiple perspectives on your experiences with CMT and may also act as inspiration and motivation to support your continued practice.

After three months of regular practice, you have completed half of your initial six-month program of CMT. During month four, you may feel ready to try a short half-day or even a full-day retreat (there is an example of this in Chapter 4 that you will be reviewing during practice month four). As you are working by yourself, you will have to organize your circumstances to accommodate a half or whole day of silence and contemplation. You may find that your local meditation center offers just such an activity, or you may organize it for yourself in your regular meditation environment. If you are working with a group or center, you will of course want to follow their format and instructions. If you are working by yourself, feel free to rotate through all of the forms you have learned so far in half-hour increments. The important thing to keep in mind during a silent retreat is that all forms of distraction (mobile phone or Internet use, checking messages, music, reading, etc.) should be avoided during the retreat period. Even when taking a break from the exercise sessions, silent, attentive focus on your internal experiences and sensations should be maintained, this is an important part of the retreat activity that tends to heighten the experiences of the retreat.

> **THE FOURTH MONTH**
>
> Review Chapter 4 of this book, paying particular attention to the exercise instructions and rationale.
>
> During month four, in addition to your regular daily meditation exercises, you will begin to experiment with and add in informal meditation sessions (see *Mindful Eating Exercise #2* and *Mindful Bathing* as examples in Chapter 4). Try the exercises provided in the book and see if you can't come up with your own versions by bringing mindfulness to some of your otherwise habitual daily activities.
>
> For daily practice during the first part of this month, pick your favorite exercise that you have learned so far (the *Conscious Breathing Exercise, Traditional Body-Scan, FAM on the Breath,* and *Mindful Movement—Walking*) and do that one exercise daily for the first two weeks. This will allow you to really focus the attention through that single exercise.
>
> At the beginning of week three, change over to the *Open Monitoring Meditation (OMM) or Mindfulness Practice* and learn this form of exercises using the guidance provided in Chapter 4. By the end of month four, you should be able to do your sessions of Mindfulness Practice without the external guidance.

For the rest of the six-month period, you should use OMM as your primary meditation style for your core daily practice. If it is yet too hard for you to maintain your attention on all of experience at once, you can alternate back and forth with the various FAM forms you have learned so far. Some will progress faster than others, so do not lose heart and be gentle (non-judgmental) with yourself.

> **MONTHS FIVE AND SIX**
>
> Review Chapter 5 of this book, paying particular attention to the exercise instructions and rationale. You can also continue to select from the references and appendix of supplementary reading material to broaden your general knowledge.
> For daily practice, focus on OMM.
> Starting in week one of this sequence, you will be adding (as your schedule permits) one or two sessions per week of both *Seated Mantra Meditation* and the *Mantra-Walking/Jogging Exercise*. These sessions can be done in addition to the daily OMM sessions or rotated as in previous months. It might be best to spend at least a week mastering the basic form of mantra meditation using the seated version before moving on to the walking/jogging versions. However, by the end of the sixth month you should be fully versed in using mantra meditation (moving or seated) and the OMM form.

Toward the end of this six-month sequence, particularly if you have not had a half-day or full-day silent retreat experience to date, you may want to engage in a full-blown multi-day retreat at an established meditation facility. Ideally, you would schedule this experience sometime in the sixth month of your training.

If you have been diligent and disciplined in learning and repeating the exercises and activities introduced so far, you have established a formal CMT practice. Congratulations! If progress has been slow or you have faltered along the way in your resolve, simply pick the practices back up and continue on. Everyone has their own individual path to follow with this kind of work, the most important thing to keep in mind is that a CMT practice is a form of self-care and self-development, so all harsh self-judgments should be relinquished in favor of a spirit of curiosity and self-cultivation. In other words, have fun with this work if you can and don't let any temporary setbacks lead to negative feelings or self-judgments.

At this point, you can carry on your practice using whichever exercises you feel have been most helpful to you. Once again, I will recommend that you try and find a group or teacher that is local to you and take advantage of it as a support system for your practice going forward. The idea of having established a regular practice is to keep it going. So, any support you can find for yourself to accomplish that goal is valuable.

The purpose of the six-month program articulated above is to establish a basic mindfulness practice that can then be maintained and expanded over time. Many of the benefits of an ongoing meditation practice explored in the earlier chapters of this book will only emerge over time with continued practice. So, as in the exercise metaphor we used above, plan to continue your practice indefinitely to garner the benefits such as stress reduction, mood-leveling, personal insight, etc.

This chapter has been addressed to the individual working alone. In the next chapter I will outline a program that can be used as the basis for a college-level, for-credit class based on the material in this book.

References

Center for Mindfulness. (2017). Center for Mindfulness Website, Silent Retreats Page. Retrieved from www.umassmed.edu/cfm/training/retreats/.

Gollwitzer, P.M., & Sheeran, P. (2006). Implementation intentions and goal achievement: A meta-analysis of effects and processes. *Advances in Experimental Social Psychology, 38,* 69–119. doi:10.1016/S0065-2601(06)38002-38001

Locke, E.A. (1968). Toward a theory of task motivation and incentives. *Organizational Behavior and Human Performance, 3*(2), 157–189. doi:10.1016/0030-5073(68)90004-90004

9

CMT IN AN INSTITUTIONAL SETTING

In the last chapter we introduced a structure for an individual College Mindfulness Training (CMT) practice. Now, we will address introducing CMT into the institutional setting, either as a support text for a mindfulness program delivered through a counseling or student services model or as the primary text for a credit-bearing undergraduate or graduate-level course covering both praxis and mindfulness as a subject matter. One of the main audiences for this book, as explained in the Introduction, is the college professor or instructor who wants to develop their own course around the subject of mindfulness. Therefore, much of the following discussion will be about creating a course outline for a college-level course based on the exercises and material presented in the first part of this book. As much of the practical and logistical information presented to the individual in the last chapter will apply to a classroom situation as well, I will repeat much of the information in the last chapter here for the benefit of the professor or instructor that wishes to develop a formal class based on this material.

CMT is more than an explication of various types of meditation and an exploration of the field of mindfulness in general. One of the goals of an institutional CMT program might be to take both the information and the exercises introduced so far and use them as the components of a credit-bearing college course. And the point of any college course based on this material is to cultivate and support the students' ongoing personal practice *after the course is complete*. So, many of the suggestions below will involve experiential learning and praxis more than subject-matter testing and evaluation; the ultimate balance between these two modes will be determined by your unique requirements. The following discussion is not intended as a complete curriculum package, but as a basis for developing your own course within the context of your institution. As an added resource for teachers endeavoring to do just that, I have included, in Appendix A, a sample of a generic course syllabus that I have developed as a guideline or starting point for customizing your own syllabus appropriate to your own academic situation.

The CMT Instructor's Personal Practice

As research for this book, I interviewed a number of mindfulness teachers and program administrators of various (mostly college-based) mindfulness programs. One of the things that they all agreed upon was that it is critical for the mindfulness teacher to have an established and ongoing *personal mindfulness practice* in order to be an effective teacher. In fact, *all* of the teachers and administrators I interviewed had a personal mindfulness practice. Some had been at it for little more than a year, while others had been meditating regularly for periods of as much as 20 and 30 years.

Holly Rogers, founder of the Koru program discussed in Chapter 3, says: "You cannot teach mindfulness unless you practice mindfulness in a fairly serious way … One thing that is really clear is that the depth of the teacher's [personal] mindfulness practice makes their teaching more effective" (Rogers, 2018).

Aurora Casta is a psychiatrist and an MBSR teacher at the Counseling and Psychology Services (CAPS) Program at the University of Pennsylvania. She has had a long-term personal meditation practice that has included a number of different styles of meditation. She is certified to teach MBSR under the guidelines of the UCSD Center for Mindfulness Program. Casta explains:

> There's a big difference on why these [mindfulness] programs work, and the teacher has to have mindfulness as part of their life. We can't be teaching something that we only know from a book … All of these mindfulness practices come out of a deep-seated knowing of what it is like to practice … so it's not something that somebody can come in and do in three weeks or two months [it takes a long-term commitment on the teacher's part].
>
> *(Casta, 2018)*

With the teacher's long-term commitment in mind, and the experiential nature of the material to be presented in any CMT program, it is highly recommended that a college-level teacher of CMT have at least one year of experience with a regular meditation practice of some form (which typically does *not* mean reading about meditation or taking physical yoga classes, but a regular practice of silent meditation of at least 30 minutes a day), or at a bare minimum completion of an eight-week MBSR training and ongoing daily practice. Many instructors that will be attracted to teaching mindfulness at the college level may well have had experience with meditation in the past which is sufficient to justify their qualification to teach CMT, as long as that instructor reacquires and maintains an ongoing practice when teaching. It is also highly recommended that a teacher of

CMT is personally involved with an outside teacher or group that can act as their mentor to answer questions and help deepen their personal practice.

Just What Is a CMT Practice?

Many people who are introduced to meditation of various forms through a class or workshop session will do the experiential work during the class or workshop but skip the homework sessions in between classes and cease meditating after the class or workshop is complete. That is a perfectly appropriate way to be introduced to meditation and mindfulness, but it is not a "practice" per se. *A mindfulness practice is an ongoing experiential activity that is intentional and sustained over time.* If the student only does the various exercises during class time and reads the chapters of this text when assigned, they will gain very few of the actual benefits of a formal mindfulness practice. In order to reap the sustained benefits attributed by the research to mindfulness meditation practices, students will need to establish a regular practice that becomes a part of their daily routine, very much like exercise becomes a regular part of a fitness routine. Therefore, one of the main objectives of any college-level mindfulness course is to help as many students as possible develop their personal practice to be a sustainable part of their lives.

The physical exercise/fitness analogy can be a useful one in explaining a CMT practice, as many college-aged students have had experience with fitness and conditioning training. This analogy can be introduced in the following way:

Let's imagine that you are starting a new personal fitness program to lose weight and tone your muscles. Your goal is to lose ten pounds and to trim down your waist by a couple of inches. You might start by looking at your diet and adjusting what you eat. You would also want to start exercising regularly, say jogging two times a week and lifting weights three times a week. So, in this example so far, you have set a goal (to lose ten pounds and trim your waistline) and planned out how you will work toward your goal over time (a diet and exercise program). Now, if you stop here, having merely set a goal and made a plan, how much success do you think you could expect? The answer, of course, is none! You have not yet done any of the actual work required to implement your plan and achieve your goals. (That would be the equivalent of reading this book but never taking the time to do any of the exercises.) Returning to our example, what if you didn't change your diet at all and only jogged once a week for a month, keeping your old lifestyle and ignoring the gym altogether. Will you have reached your goals? Again, the answer is no. In order to lose ten pounds and trim two inches off your waist, you would probably need to follow your entire plan (diet, jogging, and weights) for at least a couple of months before you could expect to see the kind of results you were hoping for. The same can be said about a CMT practice: an intention/goal, a plan for reaching that goal, and consistent work over time are all required to see the kinds of results generally promised by the research presented in the earlier chapters of this book.

Goal and Intention Setting

In the 1960s, Edwin A. Locke began research into whether or not people's goals and intentions really played any significant role in their successes at job performance. He developed a theory around goal-setting and concluded that people were more motivated and had better task performance outcomes when their goals were *difficult and challenging* rather than easy and mundane. He also found that behavioral intentions tended to regulate the kinds of choices people made, and in some cases the types of risks they were willing to take, in order to achieve specific goals (Locke, 1968). In other words, *intention is related to commitment.*

In a more recent meta-analysis of the literature on motivation and goal-setting (Gollwitzer & Sheeran, 2006), researchers acknowledged the value of basic goal-setting, à la Locke, but then went further: "[They] proposed that successful goal achievement is facilitated by a second act of willing ... termed *implementation intentions*" (2006, emphasis added). Implementation intentions, in these researcher's view, are essentially if/then plans that are triggered by certain premeditated events set by the goal maker. In our example of the fitness program above, the goal would be the same (lose weight, tighten waistline), and the implementation intentions would be the specific ways the goal-maker plans to go about doing the necessary work under various anticipated circumstances to achieve the goal. For instance, if the work plan was to jog twice and lift weights three times a week, the goal-maker might set a contingency for if it were to rain on one of her jogging days: "If it rains on my jogging day, I will do an hour on the indoor treadmill instead." Having a set of implementation intentions in place helps the goal-maker identify opportunities and possible obstacles to the execution plan and this practice tends to keep a plan of action (one of the core components of a successful mindfulness practice) from becoming interrupted or derailed by circumstances much better than a simple positive attitude (Gollwitzer & Sheeran, 2006).

In very clear language, Gollwitzer and Sheeran (2006) state that "implementation intentions appear to be effective at enhancing the likelihood of goal achievement" (p. 70). So, it would appear that successful intention setting is actually a two-step process: first setting an intention to accomplish a goal (such as engaging in an ongoing and sustained mindfulness practice); then setting specific intentions around when, where, and how you want to achieve those goals utilizing available and emerging resources.

In explaining why they thought implementation intentions seemed to be a better predictor of actual goal achievement, beyond merely having a general intention (positive attitude) to achieve a goal in the first place, Gollwitzer and Sheeran defined four general obstacles that often interfere with the goal achieving process: (1) failing to get started; (2) starting but getting derailed; (3) not calling a halt to goal striving that has become unproductive; and (4) overextending oneself. All of these situations tend to require self-regulatory behaviors to keep the goal-seeker on track, particularly over time in the quest to accomplish difficult types of meta-goals (such as a mindfulness practice); and that was where the researchers felt that the planning required by implementation intentions was useful in the ultimate acquisition of the desired goal (Gollwitzer & Sheeran, 2006, pp. 82–86).

You will want to introduce the concept of goal setting and implementation objectives early in the class process and encourage students to spend some time formulating their own goals and implementation intentions as it relates to engaging in a CMT practice. It may be worth documenting in journal form or as a short paper assignment. We will discuss journaling as a way of tracking progress and a motivation device below.

Basic Parameters of a CMT Course

The basic requirements (tools or resources) necessary to present a CMT course are minimal. Below are a list of basic resources or items that you will need to consider in preparing for a CMT course:

- A classroom or studio space that will be relatively quiet and free from interruptions during the experiential exercises (outdoor venues may be acceptable, but on most college campuses there is a great deal of noise and other possible distractors, so a secure indoor venue is generally preferable).
- An open space, such as a movement or dance studio is optimal, however, in a classroom already filled with desks or fixed seating, you can adapt the exercises for a sitting position, or, where it is possible, move the desks out of the way to provide enough floor space for movement or lying down as necessary. The space is important, and can be strongly supportive of the CMT exercises, however, all of the exercises can be adapted or elected to conform to the space you have available.
- If sitting or lying on the floor is possible in your physical space, you may wish to provide (or require students to bring) appropriate padding: pillows for sitting, perhaps a yoga pad and some rolled up blankets to support head and knees when lying down. There are several different ways to make sure that your students will be comfortable and adequately supported during work sessions, but the important thing is to have thought through and solved these issues by the time of the first class as every class session will involve some experiential work.
- An egg timer or (non-ticking) alarm clock for timing practice sessions is required. It is best to avoid using a cellphone for this purpose as even vibration alerts from a muted phone are distracting, however, if you have no other option, a cellphone is acceptable as long as you mute (or turn off completely) the notifications function during class time.
- For guided meditations, you will most likely want to narrate the guidance by simply reading the guidance scripts in the text (this may require a little

practice to optimize the timing). You can also pre-record the guidance scripts using a tape recorder. However, reading the guidance aloud allows you to time out the exercises, and make adjustments as necessary and thus is generally the more flexible method. Try to avoid using cellphones for playback for the same reasons noted above.
- If you are assigning any apps or gadgets to your students, make sure they have had adequate time to acquire and install them. As a general rule, apps and gadgets should mostly be used outside of the classroom as adjunct resources and not as a classroom activity where your direct guidance will be the most useful.

The point of preparing your space and equipment (if any) in advance is to limit any distractions or waste of time during class sessions. However, unexpected events and inconveniences do occasionally occur and so, as with thinking through implementation intentions above, you might do well to consider various alternative plans if your classroom environment is not ideal or wholly controllable.

Below, I will lay out a basic outline for a one-semester CMT class. This outline will assume two one-hour-and-fifteen-minute class sessions per week and the daily assignment of experiential homework on off-days, although it can be altered to any class schedule you have available in your particular circumstances. In communicating the course requirements to students, it is important to emphasize in a clear manner that attendance and regular outside homework sessions are the major *requirement* for this class and without regular attendance and out-of-class participation in the exercises, the student will not successfully complete the course. It is important to be stringent about these requirements as the majority of the learning will be experiential and if the students do not actually do the work during the course of the semester, they will not gain proficiency in the skills.

In general, it is best to start CMT with Focused Attention Meditation (FAM) and then move to Open Monitoring (mindfulness) Meditation (OMM) practice when the students have stabilized their ability to hold attention steady in a focused fashion for at least a few minutes at a time. In the model below, we will start with FAM practices and move into OMM techniques gradually during the semester.

THE FIRST FOUR WEEKS: EXERCISES AND ASSIGNMENTS

Class One: After the instructor has made introductory remarks and established the ground rules for the CMT class (such as no powered-on mobile devices in the room), the students are introduced to *The Watch Exercise* and *Mindful Eating Exercise #1* (see Chapter 1), both of which should be executed with the minimum of upfront explanation. The goal of this abrupt introduction to the experiential work is for the students to experience their current level and state of consciousness (and control of attention) in a visceral and direct way. After these exercises are complete, a more general discussion may ensue, including a brief introduction of each student (to begin to facilitate group process, which will be an important aspect of the CMT course dynamic) and why they elected to take this course, as well as individual observations and reactions to the exercises. If the class size is larger than 12–14 students, you may want to break up the discussion groups into multiple smaller units. Generally, groups of between eight and 14 work best for class discussions of this sort.

Reading assignments for the first week (given after these initial exercises) include the first part of Chapter 1 through the *Emerging Adulthood and College Stress* section (to be completed before the second class period). Chapter 1 gives a brief introduction to the topic of mindfulness and stress as a factor in emerging adulthood and can be discussed in the second class meeting. The ongoing journaling assignment should be introduced with the understanding that it will begin in week two of the class (after some more exercises have been introduced in class two and homework has been assigned).

In the second class period, the teacher will introduce the instructions for the *Conscious Breathing* exercise (Chapter 1) and guide the exercise for approximately 30 minutes. Conscious Breathing will be assigned as the homework exercise on off-days until the next class meeting (pre-recorded audio files with the instructions can be prepared by the instructor for the use by the students until they are comfortable that they know the instructions and can guide themselves without narration). Class discussion of both the experiential exercise and assigned reading should follow each session. The rest of Chapter 1, which includes the instructions for the *Traditional Body Scan*, should be assigned for reading before the start of the second week's classes.

The experiential homework exercises are assigned for each off-class day throughout the semester (excluding weekends). So, for instance, if classes are held on Tuesdays and Thursday (as in this model), then homework would be due on Mondays, Wednesdays, and Fridays each week. The students are expected to log each session, the length of each session, what time of day or evening it was engaged, and any personal reflections in their meditation journal. Meditation journals are generally a tracking device and mode of honor-system documentation that is reviewed weekly by the instructor but is not part of the formal grading (unless the journal indicates that the student has not done a sufficient amount of the experiential homework). If students are indicating in their journals that they are having difficulty completing the homework assignments, this offers the instructor the opportunity to work with the student to rectify any deficiencies or help them develop a custom strategy for inculcating the work into their individual schedule. Depending on the instructor's skill-set and available digital resources, the journaling activity may be submitted digitally over email or other instructor/student communication platform available at the particular institution. The key thing with the journaling activity is to keep it simple for the students so that it serves the function of giving them a structure for their practice without becoming an undue burden and interfering with practice time.

As a general instruction, it should be made clear that students in this class are expected to log five meditation sessions per week (inclusive of the in-class work) in order to meet class requirements. If they miss a session during the week, they can make it up over the weekend, the goal being a *total* of five sessions of practice every week during the course of the semester. This experiential practice is important both because it is the singular key for cultivating mindfulness in daily life and because the practice time represents the major portion of course work, as writing assignments and traditional testing are minimal (depending on the requirements of the individual institution for credit-bearing courses, this balance can be adjusted, but the experiential work will always be a required element).

During week two, start each class with a 15-minute *Conscious Breathing* session as a type of warm-up or centering activity, explaining that this provides a convenient break between what was going on before class and the important work at hand by bringing everyone's attention into the present moment through this simple exercise.

In week two, we introduce the Traditional Body Scan as a 30-miniute guided meditation as the centerpiece of each class. The guided version of the Traditional Body Scan will follow Conscious Breathing each day and be the off-day assignment for the week as well.

At the end of the first class of week two, students are assigned the first part of Chapter 2 of this book: *Attention and Distraction in the Digital Age* (to be discussed in the next class period).

By the beginning of week three, the students should be fairly comfortable with both the Conscious Breathing and Traditional Body Scan exercises and potentially be able to do them without narrative guidance (although it may take another week using the pre-recorded guidance for the Body Scan as it is more complex). Use the first class period of week three to check in and answer any questions the students may have about these exercises. You may also want to allow some time for group discussions as the group process dynamic is often helpful in engaging students with the work throughout the semester.

The reading assignment (given in the first class session of week three for review later in the week) is the second half of Chapter 2, *Focused Attention Meditation (FAM) on the Breath*. And, FAM on the Breath will be the primary classroom and homework assignment for the week. In this week, the instructor may want to facilitate a discussion of the basic qualities and guidelines for seated (non-moving) FAM, including the likelihood of distractions and non-judgmently bringing the attention back to the breath and beginning again. Counting or Labeling Breaths can be introduced in either class session but,

> once introduced, should become the primary mode of FAM on the Breath sessions for at least the next month to allow for students to start to stabilize their attention control. After the majority of students report improving attentional control, they can be allowed to drop the counting or labeling activity, but in the majority of cases, counting or labeling is helpful in establishing a seated FAM practice.
>
> Week four is a continuation of practice with the three exercises introduced so far (with an emphasis on FAM on the Breath). Reading and discussion for this week can be the first half of Chapter 3, including MBSR, Koru, and CMT protocols. Save the *Mindful Movement—Walking* exercise for introduction in week five. Class discussion can also investigate the experiential differences between guided and silent versions of the exercises, usefulness of counting of the breaths, and any questions the students have about their practice so far.

During the first half of this semester, the students have learned to internalize the instructions and forms of the basic FAM exercises. They may have expressed frustration and even personal struggle with their thought streams and inability to focus, particularly at the beginning of class; but by the end of the first few weeks, they should be starting to show signs of calming mental activity during practice and a general ability to settle into the various exercises with less effort. To the degree that there is frustration or minor distress, students should be encouraged to engage in CMT practice in a non-judgmental fashion, simply following the instructions and gently leading the mind back to the focus of the exercise when it wanders. A certain amount of struggle is expected and is actually part of the process, so all reasonable encouragement and support should be offered. Some students may report that the meditation practice seems to be "making their thoughts race." This is a normal reaction and usually a function of becoming aware of how fragmented and erratic the thought processes already are. The instructor can explain that the students should expect for it to take a substantial amount of time and work to see noticeable improvement in control over their attention function and a general calming of mental "noise." Instructors can assure the students that with practice they will become better at staying focused and eventually the degree of fragmentation and fervor of their thoughts and emotions will stabilize.

The general point of focusing on FAM training in the first few weeks is to gain at least a minimal amount of control over the attentional function before advancing into other forms of CMT practice with less structure, such as OMM.

> ## THE SECOND FOUR WEEKS
>
> It is often best, particularly while still establishing an individual CMT practice, to avoid too much variety and instead become deeply familiar and

comfortable with the practices that will eventually become the core work of CMT practice. Therefore, during this part of the semester, students will mainly be focusing on the exercises they have learned so far (and *Mindful Movement —Walking*, introduced below) as their primary experiential activities. As a warm-up in class, instructors can use a shortened version of either the *Traditional Body Scan* or *Conscious Breathing* exercises, perhaps for the first ten or 15 minutes of each class session, and then settle into *FAM on the Breath* (with counting) or *Mindful Movement—Walking* as the main activity for this entire period. This will allow students to deepen their concentration during the exercises and become effortlessly adept with these exercises in silence without need of narrative guidance. Journaling activity should continue throughout.

In the first class session of week five, the instructor will introduce the guided version of *Mindful Movement—Walking* (see Chapter 3). With this exercise, the students have learned all of the basic FAM exercises that make up CMT practice. As stated above, they will continue these for the next four weeks before they are introduced to the more free-form Open Monitoring Meditation (OMM) in the second half of the semester. Week five reading and discussion can include all of Chapter 4 (except the OMM exercises at the end). These topics include informal mindfulness practice and exercises, mindfulness of technology, and silent retreats.

In week six, the students are assigned a short reflection paper (due in week seven) that describes their experiences with one of the informal mindfulness exercises from Chapter 4: *Mindful Eating Exercise #2* (a mindful meal), *Mindful Bathing*, or *Mindfulness of Technology*. In-class and homework exercises continue with the students picking their own favorite FAM exercises to focus on for their off-day homework.

In weeks seven and eight, students are assigned to focus exclusively on silent FAM on the Breath as their homework exercise. By the end of the eighth week, those students who are comfortable doing so are invited to drop the counting or labeling and simply observe the pure process of breathing, both in and out, without any added mental construction. It can be explained that the mind will very likely still wander and the attention will still need to be gently but firmly returned to the breath whenever that distraction is noticed, but by concentrating on the pure experience of breathing, without counting, the attention function will eventually become strengthened and meditation sessions may begin to feel more relaxing and even refreshing.

Reading and discussion in weeks seven and eight are at the instructor's discretion. They can be drawn from materials listed in Appendix B, or from supplemental reading sources such as Ken Wilber's *Integral Meditation: Mindfulness as a Way to Grow Up, Wake Up, and Show Up in Your Life* (2016) (the example I will use in the sample syllabus in Appendix A). Or weekly reading assignments can be suspended for a time in favor of discussing the students' experiences with the exercises themselves.

> In any case, students should continue to track their daily work (for a total of five sessions per week, including in-class sessions), and periodically submit them for un-graded review.

By the end of the first eight weeks, the students should have established a regular pattern of weekly meditation sessions that has become easy to maintain and, hopefully, a desirable and valued activity in their day. However, some students may have exhibited significant resistance toward the work by this time. In such cases, the student has often dropped the class by this time (and should be allowed to do so). Some people are simply not suited to mindfulness training work and so some attrition is to be expected.

The majority of students, however, will probably start to report that their minds are calming from their original chaotic state of roiling thought and attaining periods of quiet, focused silence where it becomes easier, even joyful, to stay focused on the object of meditation (breath, sensations, movement). These periods of stable focus will start to become longer and longer. If students feel their progress has been slow but they are not heavily resisting the work as described above, they should continue to be supported because each person's progress will be different. They should be encouraged to keep doing the practices regularly and with discipline. The only exception to this is if a student is experiencing serious distress or mental disturbance. If this is the case, and it does not appear to be mere resistance to the practice in general but actual upsetting mental states, it may be necessary for that student to *discontinue the program*. A serious meditation practice will often have moments of physical and mental discomfort, resistance, and doubts; these are all part of the normal challenge of consciousness work. However, significant mental upset, panic attacks (particularly if sustained), auditory or visual hallucinations, depression, ruminative thinking that does not stop between sessions, or other noticeably disruptive psychological symptoms are all potential side effects that need to be understood and resolved before continuing regular meditation practice for any student. These types of incidents are rare but are possible with a small percentage of the population.

WEEKS NINE THROUGH TWELVE

In the first class of week nine, students will learn, through the guided version, OMM or mindfulness meditation (see the last part of Chapter 4). OMM will be the homework meditation for this entire week. Reading assignment, if any, can come from supplemental reading sources selected by the instructor.

In week ten, we introduce Mantra Meditation (a form of FAM that takes as its object of attention a word or phrase, see Chapter 5). Each class session and homework session in this week should include both OMM and Mantra

Meditation work. If the environment is suitable, the class could be taken outside and engage in a group Mantra Walk (see Chapter 5).

In week eleven, we continue to alternate or combine both OMM and Mantra, and homework can include Mindful Exercise (see Chapter 5). During week eleven, the class can also discuss the silent retreat material in Chapter 5, in anticipation of the upcoming retreat experience (see below).

In week twelve, in addition to continuing OMM and Mantra practice, the class should plan to take part in either a half-day (three to four hours) or full-day (six to eight hours) silent retreat experience. The retreat can take place anytime between week twelve and the end of the semester depending on scheduling, facilities availability, etc.

Logistically the silent retreat experience might well need to be scheduled on a weekend and should be announced as a required part of the course at the beginning of the semester so that students can make appropriate arrangements with their schedules. Also, the silent retreat setting might represent a good time to invite an experienced outside meditation teacher to help facilitate the retreat and be available to answer student questions about meditation practice in general. (This suggestion is, of course, optional and subject to available resources.) A silent retreat is not absolutely essential to the course, but it is a very valuable experience and one that often helps meditation students culminate their work todate, so, if the resources are available, it is a highly recommended element of a well-rounded CMT program.

During the retreat day, the students and instructors will observe total verbal silence, except for instructions necessary to direct the meditation sessions. The entire experience should be focused on various forms of FAM and OMM work. Formal sessions can be structured to rotate between passive and movement techniques to avoid physical discomfort from sitting too long. Meal breaks, if there are any, are taken in silence and are to be conducted as a mindful eating exercise.

During the retreat, there should be no cellphones or digital devices of any kind throughout the day, even (or especially) on breaks; nor should there be any television, reading, or music allowed. Silence means *silence* and is an important ingredient of the work for the day.

At the end of the mini-retreat, the class can gather as a group and slowly re-engage in a discussion about individual experiences throughout the day. Students and instructors should take turns speaking and be mindful of the others who have shared the experience instead of merely jumping back in to normal or overlapping conversation cadence. Sometimes a ritualized "talking stick" is used to control the flow of the discussion and remind all participants to remain mindful even during this debriefing session.

If the class is able to arrange a half-day or full-day silent retreat, a reaction paper of 4–5 pages may be assigned. Alternatively, a reaction paper to some

> element of FAM or OMM training could also be assigned and made due by the end of the semester.

By this point, the students have established a basic meditation practice and experimented with a number of forms including FAM, OMM, informal, and mantra meditation, and should be mostly comfortable with self-guiding all of these exercises. If at this point students have questions or concerns, the remaining weeks of the semester are a good time to address those questions and reinforce the basic exercises instructions where necessary.

During their meditation sessions, they will most likely still report distracting thoughts and feelings, as thinking never actually stops (until death). For the most part, mental disturbance and distraction should begin to come under individual control and "settle" or "calm," so that there are periods where it seems that thought has actually ceased. Students will probably start to look forward to their daily meditation sessions. They may proselytize about the practice to their friends and fellow students. They may want to research other forms of meditative practice on their own and possibly locate and join outside meditation groups.

> **THE FINAL WEEKS**
>
> As mentioned above, at this point all students should have developed a regular basic meditation practice. However, as everyone is different, and will have different personal preferences, in these final weeks, the students should be encouraged to pick their favorite form of either FAM or OMM and concentrate on that single exercise as their homework for the rest of the semester. This will allow them to more deeply explore the form of meditation training that most appeals to them and build a momentum in their practice that is more likely to carry forward after the class has ended.
>
> Chapters 6, 7, and 8 can be assigned at the instructor's discretion and make up the core of class discussions for the rest of the semester. The instructor may wish to purchase, as part of the class supplies, any of the apps and gadgets described in Chapter 6 so as to give the students a chance to experience these technologies first-hand (without having to bear the expense themselves). Once the students have completed the material in this book up through Chapter 8, readings can either be suspended or assigned from appropriate supplementary reading source (see Appendix B). If a final paper is required, these final weeks are a good time for that assignment.

This discussion has been a general outline only and much adaptation may be required to fit your own institutional situation. To save the individual instructor some work, and as a starting place for formal course development, I have used the information above as the content for a sample course syllabus (see Appendix A).

Conclusions

This book is for both college-aged emerging adults interested in adopting a meditation practice as well as understanding the mindfulness phenomenon in general, and college professors and instructors (or counselors, staff, mental health professionals, etc.) who want to teach a basic course in mindfulness training directly germane to a college-aged audience. If you have read and used this book up until this point, you will have established a basic mindfulness practice (or helped others to do so), to the degree that you have actually executed and repeated the experiential exercises over time. By the end of either example timeframes proposed (six-month or an academic semester), you may be experiencing certain benefits of a regular mindfulness practice, and there may be other benefits yet to emerge if you keep your practice up. Some of the changes you notice may include: improved attentional control and executive function, being more present "in the moment" and less likely to project into the future, reduced anxiety, reduced social anxiety, a higher tolerance for uncertainty, a more relaxed general mood, and a broadened horizon of awareness. You may find your relationships improving. You may be able to sleep better. You may be able to deal with stressful situations better or with more equanimity. Each person is different and so you will be the judge as to whether your own practice of these exercises has helped you, in what ways, and to what extent.

You are, of course, encouraged to continue to practice your CMT program after your class ends or you have completed the sequence outlined herein. It will all come down to what value you have found in this work. At this point you may be interested in finding a group or a teacher to deepen your practice. Or you may set the practice down for a time and return to it later in life. In any case, whatever growth you experience from this point on as a result of CMT will begin with an awareness of your very next breath … and this breath … and this breath …

References

Casta, A. (2018, December 15). Aurora Casta interview by K. Page.
Gollwitzer, P.M., & Sheeran, P. (2006). Implementation intentions and goal achievement: A meta-analysis of effects and processes. *Advances in Experimental Social Psychology*, *38*, 69–119. doi:10.1016/S0065-2601(06)38002-38001
Locke, E.A. (1968). Toward a theory of task motivation and incentives. *Organizational Behavior and Human Performance*, *3*(2), 157–189. doi:10.1016/0030-5073(68)90004-90004
Rogers, H.B. (2018, April 1). Holly Rogers interview by K. Page.
Wilber, K. (2016). *Integral meditation: Mindfulness as a way to grow up, wake up, and show up in your life* (first edition). Boulder: Shambhala.

APPENDIX A

Sample CMT Course Syllabus

Following is a simple example of a course syllabus for a credit-bearing course in CMT. If you are a professor or instructor developing a course in mindfulness training, the following may represent a starting point for you to begin developing your own syllabus customized to your institution's standards. (For a general discussion of course structure and content, see Chapter 9.) This model is structured on a two-day-a-week, one-hour-and-fifteen-minute class-length schedule. This model can also be adapted to a three-day-a-week structure.

Instructor Information: This section will include instructor(s) name(s), contact information, preferred modes of communication, office hours, website and social media information, etc.

Course Description: College Mindfulness Training (CMT) introduces the practices of secular mindfulness meditation training in a context appropriate to college-aged students. In this course we look at the term "mindfulness" in three distinct ways. First, as a form or style of meditation; mindfulness as a resultant state of consciousness cultivated by certain types of meditation practice; and finally, as a socio-cultural movement proliferating throughout Western culture, in particular in the form of academically sponsored programs and initiatives.

Concerns over stress and performance, anxiety, and depression are all on the rise in the college environment as are the number of students seeking counseling help for these maladies. In the CMT course, we will look at some of the research defining college stress and research on mindfulness practice and other forms of meditation that can offer some relief for that stress and related complaints.

A central feature of CMT is *experiential learning* through regular practice of various forms of meditation. In the course, we will introduce several different types of meditative practice, including Focused Attention Meditation (FAM), Open Monitoring Meditation (OMM), and both formal and informal ways to engage in the various practices. Homework for this course is mandatory and will rely heavily on daily out-of-class individual practice of these experiential activities. Attendance at all class sessions is mandatory and represents a large part of your grade.

Purpose of the Course and Learning Goals

The CMT course is intended to introduce both the field of and an experiential engagement with mindfulness meditation. During the course of the semester, you will:

- Learn and practice various forms of Focused Attention Meditation (the body-scan, consciousness of breath, mindful movement, and others).
- Learn and practice Open Monitoring Meditation (often called "mindfulness" or "insight" meditation).
- Learn and practice in both formal and informal modes.
- Keep a meditation journal to track your progress.
- Explore various topics of interest or concern to college-aged "emerging adults" and discover ways that meditation practice can help with some of these issues.
- Review the research that supports the usefulness of a regular meditation practice.
- Be introduced to several programs and initiatives in the "mindfulness industry" and develop a general understanding of what kinds of jobs are emerging in this multi-billion-dollar field.
- Be introduced to several apps and technology platforms that purport to support various types of mindfulness practice.
- Develop your own customized CMT program that you can continue with after the class is complete.

Some of the common questions we will explore in this course, include:

- What is meditation and what does it do?
- How can meditation practice help with the stressors common to college life?
- What is MBSR?
- What is Koru?
- What are some basic forms of Focused Attention Meditation (FAM)?
- What are some of the basic forms of Open Monitoring Meditation (OMM)?
- What sorts of apps and technology are available to support meditation practice?
- How do I develop an individual meditation practice?
- What types of meditation practice are right for me?
- What kinds of jobs are emerging from the mindfulness field?

This course is intended to help prepare you for:

- A lifetime individual meditation practice.
- The stresses of your own college career.
- Jobs in the field of meditation services and mindfulness research.

Readings and Class Materials

Required Text: *College mindfulness training* (Routledge, 2019) by Kevin Page.

Supplemental Text: *Integral meditation: Mindfulness as a way to grow up, wake up, and show up in your life* (Shambhala, 2016) by Ken Wilber.

Recommended Texts

Barbezat, D., & Bush, M. (2014). Contemplative practices in higher education: Powerful methods to transform teaching and learning. San Francisco: Jossey-Bass.

Goleman, D., & Davidson, R.J. (2017). Altered traits: Science reveals how meditation changes your mind, brain, and body. New York: Avery.

Kabat-Zinn, J. (2005). Wherever you go, there you are: Mindfulness meditation in everyday life. New York: Hyperion.

McCown, D., Reibel, D., & Micozzi, M.S. (2010). Teaching mindfulness: A practical guide for clinicians and educators. New York and London: Springer.

Ragoonaden, K. (2015). Mindful teaching and learning: Developing a pedagogy of well-being. Lanham: Lexington Books.

Rogers, H. (2016). The mindful twenty-something: Life skills to handle stress … and everything else. Oakland: New Harbinger Publications, Inc.

Schonert-Reichl, K. (2016). Handbook of mindfulness in education: Integrating theory and research into practice. New York: Springer.

Shy, Y. (2017). What now? Meditation for your twenties and beyond. Berkeley: Parallax Press.

Audio recordings of the guidance instructions most exercises will be made available for online streaming and homework practice.

Students may want to consider the (optional) purchase of a meditation cushion and pad, as well as a yoga mat, for home use.

Course Policies and Expectations

This course is primarily experiential. The majority of your grade will be based on class attendance and participation and the successful completion of the homework assignments. Therefore, *attendance at all scheduled class sessions is mandatory*. Two tardies will be counted as an absence. Only legitimate family or health emergencies with written doctor's excuses will be allowed to count as excused absences.

It is very important that you are *on time* to class as late entry (or early exit) will interfere with the experiential work of the entire class.

There is a complete ban on all electronic devices (cellphones, tablets, laptops, and wearables such as smart watches or earbuds, etc.) in this class. All electronic devices must be powered down and stowed in your backpack, *not in pockets or on your person*. The reason for this is that even silent vibrating alarms and alerts are distracting and disruptive to the work of this class and will not be tolerated.

This class operates on the honor system. You will be expected to keep a regular journal of your homework assignments. These journals will be handed in, from time to time, and evaluated for the constancy of your homework participation, although they will not be graded, as such. (NOTE TO INSTRUCTORS: Where the technology is available, journal assignments may be submitted electronically; this will depend on your institution's available resources.)

[Include any other institution-specific policies here.]

Grading

As stated before, this class is primarily one based on *experiential learning* and operated on the honor system (we trust that you will live up to your commitments). The majority of your grade will be derived from regular class attendance and participation, as well as physically *doing* your homework assignments on non-class days (and tracking those assignments in a personal journal that is subject to review by the instructor at regular intervals). Class exercises and homework assignments will mostly consist of different types of meditation practices and explorations of your own consciousness in ways that require your direct participation for between 15 and 30 minutes per session. This material cannot be learned by reading but must be experienced directly by you. In addition to the experiential work, there will be light reading assignments and two short reaction papers due during the semester. Below are the grading guidelines your instructor will follow.

Class attendance, participation, and experiential homework assignments: 60% of your grade.

Attendance and participation at the half-day silent retreat: 15% of your grade.

Written reaction papers and reading assignments: 25% of your grade.

Additionally, the instructor may, from time to time, make extra-credit opportunities available.

Tentative Class Schedule

This class meets on Tuesdays and Thursdays throughout the semester. In addition, there is a half-day silent retreat that will be offered later in the semester. Please be cognizant of the dates available for the silent retreat experience and notify the instructor as early as possible if you will not be able to participate.

The following schedule is tentative and may change without notice at the instructor's discretion.

January, Week One

Tuesday:

Discussion: Introductions and class expectations. Ongoing journaling assignment is introduced (to commence in week two).

Experiential exercises: The Watch Exercise and *Mindful Eating Exercise #1*.

Reading assignment (due for next class): *College Mindfulness Training* (CMT book), first part of Chapter 1 (through the *Emerging Adulthood and College Stress* section).

Thursday:

Discussion: Mindfulness, definitions. College stress.

Experiential exercises: Conscious Breathing (instructor guided).

Reading assignment (due for next class): CMT book, the rest of Chapter 1, which includes the instructions for the *Traditional Body Scan*.

Homework assignment: Conscious Breathing (utilizing pre-recorded guidance script).

January, Week Two

Tuesday:

Discussion: Responses to experiential exercise, *Conscious Breathing*; issues, difficulties, value of journaling activity.

Experiential exercises: Conscious Breathing (warm-up) and *Traditional Body Scan* (instructor guided).

Reading assignment (due for next class): first part of Chapter 2 of CMT book: *Attention and Distraction in the Digital Age* (up to *Focused Attention Meditation (FAM) on the Breath*).

Homework assignment: Traditional Body Scan (utilizing pre-recorded guidance script).

Thursday:

Discussion: Attention and distraction; responses to *Traditional Body Scan* homework.

Experiential exercises: Conscious Breathing (warm-up) and *Traditional Body Scan* (instructor guided).

Reading assignment (due for next class): CMT book, the rest of Chapter 2, which includes the instructions for *Focused Attention Meditation (FAM) on the Breath* and *Counting or Labeling Breaths*.

Homework assignment: Traditional Body Scan (utilizing pre-recorded guidance script).

January, Week Three

Tuesday:

Discussion: Body Scan homework; reading on FAM exercise; **Meditation Journals due for evaluation**.

Experiential exercises: Conscious Breathing (warm-up) and *Focused Attention Meditation (FAM) on the Breath* (instructor guided).

Homework assignment: FAM on the Breath (utilizing pre-recorded guidance script).

Thursday:

Discussion: Responses to experiential exercises; adding counting or labeling breaths to homework.

Experiential exercises: Conscious Breathing (warm-up) and *FAM on the Breath* (instructor guided, adding counting breaths).

Reading assignment (due for next class): CMT book, first half of Chapter 3, including MBSR, Koru, and CMT protocols.

Homework assignment: FAM on the Breath (utilizing pre-recorded guidance script).

January, Week Four

Tuesday:

Discussion: MBSR, Koru, and CMT protocols.

Experiential exercises: Conscious Breathing (warm-up) and *FAM on the Breath* (instructor guided, counting breaths).

Homework assignment: FAM on the Breath (internalized—silent, self-guided).

Thursday:

Discussion: Experiential differences between guided and silent versions of the exercises.

Experiential exercises: Conscious Breathing (warm-up) and *FAM on the Breath* (silent, self-guided).

Reading assignment (due for next class): CMT book, the rest of Chapter 3, the *Mindful Movement—Walking* exercise

Homework assignment: FAM on the Breath (internalized—silent, self-guided).

February, Week One

Tuesday:

Discussion: Reading assignment and experiential work; **Meditation Journals due for evaluation**.

Experiential exercises: FAM on the Breath (warm-up) and *Mindful Movement—Walking* exercise.

Reading assignment (due for next class): CMT book, first part of Chapter 4 (through the *Silent Retreat* section).

Homework assignment: Mindful Movement—Walking exercise

Thursday:

Discussion: Reading assignment (formal/informal practices, mindfulness of technology) and experiential work.

Experiential exercises: FAM on the Breath (warm-up) and *Mindful Movement—Walking* exercise.

Homework assignment: Mindful Movement—Walking exercise; select one *informal practice*.

February, Week Two

Tuesday:

Discussion: Silent retreats; informal practice; **assign reaction paper**: informal practice or mindfulness of technology (2–3 pages, due by beginning of class next Thursday).

Experiential exercises: Mindful Movement—Walking exercise (warm-up) and *FAM on the Breath*.

Homework assignment: FAM on the Breath; informal practices as research for reaction paper.

Thursday:

Discussion: Experiential exercises; questions on paper.

Experiential exercises: Mindful Movement—Walking exercise (warm-up) and *FAM on the Breath*.

Homework assignment: FAM on the Breath; work on reaction paper.

February, Week Three

Tuesday:

Discussion: Experiential exercises; questions on paper.

Experiential exercises: Mindful Movement—Walking exercise (warm-up) and *FAM on the Breath*.

Homework assignment: FAM on the Breath; work on reaction paper.

Thursday:

Discussion: **Reaction papers due**.

Experiential exercises: Mindful Movement—Walking exercise (warm-up) and *FAM on the Breath*.

Homework assignment: FAM on the Breath.

February, Week Four

Tuesday:

Discussion: Experiential exercises; **Meditation Journals due for evaluation**.

Experiential exercises: Mindful Movement—Walking exercise (warm-up) and *FAM on the Breath.*
Reading assignment: assigned by instructor.
Homework assignment: FAM on the Breath.
Thursday:
Discussion: Experiential exercises, dropping the counting or labeling of breaths in favor of bare attention on following the breath; reading assignment.
Experiential exercises: Mindful Movement—Walking exercise (warm-up) and *FAM on the Breath.*
Reading assignment: assigned by instructor.
Homework assignment: FAM on the Breath.

March, Week One

Tuesday:
Discussion: Reading assignment; experiential exercises.
Experiential exercises: Mindful Movement—Walking exercise (warm-up) and *Open Monitoring Meditation (OMM) or Mindfulness Practice* (instructor guided).
Reading assignment (due for next class): CMT book, last part of Chapter 4 (instructions for *Open Monitoring Meditation (OMM) or Mindfulness Practice*).
Homework assignment: Open Monitoring Meditation (OMM) (using pre-recorded guidance).
Thursday:
Discussion: experiential exercises.
Experiential exercises: Mindful Movement—Walking exercise (warm-up) and *Open Monitoring Meditation (OMM) or Mindfulness Practice* (instructor guided).
Reading assignment (due after Spring Break): CMT book, first part of Chapter 5 (through *Seated Mantra Meditation*).
Homework assignment: Open Monitoring Meditation (OMM) (using pre-recorded guidance).

March, Week Two

Tuesday:
Spring Break
Extra Credit: Continue to journal daily OMM sessions over Spring Break for extra credit.
Thursday:
Spring Break
Extra Credit: Continue to journal daily OMM sessions over Spring Break for extra credit.

March, Week Three

Tuesday:
Discussion: Progress with all exercises to-date; reading assignment (mindful exercise and mantra meditation); **Meditation Journals due for evaluation**.
Experiential exercises: Mindful Movement—Walking exercise (warm-up) and *Seated Mantra Meditation*.
Reading assignment (due for next class): CMT book, last part of Chapter 5 (*Mantra Workout*).
Homework assignment: Seated Mantra Meditation.
Thursday:
Discussion: Responses to *Seated Mantra Meditation*; reading assignment on Mantra Workout.
Experiential exercises: Group Mantra-Walking/Jogging Exercise (outside on exercise track).
Reading assignment: Assigned by instructor.
Homework assignment: Alternate days between *OMM* (silent, self-guided) and *Mantra Meditation* (either seated or exercise versions per individual preference).

March, Week Four

Tuesday:
Discussion: experiential work/progress; silent retreat activity.
Experiential exercises: Mantra Meditation (warm-up) and *OMM* (silent, self-guided).
Reading assignment: Assigned by instructor.
Homework assignment: Choose between *OMM* and *Mantra Meditation* (either seated or exercise versions per individual preference).
Thursday:
Discussion: Experiential work.
Experiential exercises: Mantra Meditation (warm-up) and *OMM* (silent, self-guided).
Reading assignment (due by first class next week): CMT book, Chapter 6 (*Apps and Gadgets*).
Homework assignment: Choose between *OMM* and *Mantra Meditation* (either seated or exercise versions per individual preference).

April, Week One

Tuesday:
Discussion: Apps and Gadgets; **assignment of reaction paper to upcoming silent retreat** (final project); **Meditation Journals due for evaluation**.
Experiential exercises: Mindful Movement—Walking exercise (warm-up) and *OMM*.
Reading assignment: Assigned by instructor.

Homework assignment: Choose between *OMM* and *Mantra Meditation* (either seated or exercise versions per individual preference).

Thursday:

Discussion: Reading assignment.

Experiential exercises: Mindful Movement—Walking exercise (warm-up) and *OMM*.

Reading assignment (due by first class next week): CMT book: Chapter 7 (*Programs and Initiatives*).

Homework assignment: Choose between *OMM* and *Mantra Meditation* (either seated or exercise versions per individual preference).

Friday, 6–10pm—First silent retreat opportunity (location to be announced). You are required to attend one of the two available retreat sessions to complete this course. If you cannot make either opportunity, please see instructor as soon as possible to discuss options.

April, Week Two

Tuesday:

Discussion: Programs and Initiatives, potential job opportunities, future research opportunities.

Experiential exercises: Mindful Movement—Walking exercise (warm-up) and *OMM*.

Reading assignment: Assigned by instructor.

Homework assignment: Choose between *OMM* and *Mantra Meditation* (either seated or exercise versions per individual preference).

Thursday:

Discussion: Reading assignment.

Experiential exercises: Mindful Movement—Walking exercise (warm-up) and *OMM*.

Reading assignment: Assigned by instructor.

Homework assignment: Choose between *OMM* and *Mantra Meditation* (either seated or exercise versions per individual preference).

Saturday, 10am–2pm—Second silent retreat opportunity (location to be announced). You are *required* to attend one of the two available retreat sessions to complete this course. If you cannot make either opportunity, please see instructor as soon as possible to discuss options.

April, Week Three

Tuesday:

Discussion: Reading assignment; silent retreat experiences.

Experiential exercises: Mindful Movement—Walking exercise (warm-up) and *OMM*.

Reading assignment (due by first class next week): CMT book: Chapter 8 (*Individual CMT Practice*).

Homework assignment: Choose your favorite form of either FAM or OMM and concentrate on that single exercise as your homework for the rest of the semester.

Thursday:

Discussion: Individual CMT practice.

Experiential exercises: Mindful Movement—Walking exercise (warm-up) and *OMM*.

Reading assignment: No reading assignment leaving time to work on final paper.

Homework assignment: Choose your favorite form of either FAM or OMM and concentrate on that single exercise as your homework for the rest of the semester.

April, Week Four

Tuesday:

Discussion: Final paper; class evaluations; **Meditation Journals due for evaluation**.

Experiential exercises: Mindful Movement—Walking exercise (warm-up) and *OMM*.

Reading assignment: No reading assignment leaving time to work on final paper.

Homework assignment: Work on final paper.

Thursday:

Discussion: Maintaining a CMT practice after course completion/local resources.

Experiential exercises: Mindful Movement—Walking exercise (warm-up) and *OMM*. *Final paper due and closing ceremonies*.

APPENDIX B

Research Articles and Book Resources

Following is an extensive list of research articles and books related to mindfulness, meditation, and the attention function. Many of these references have been cited in the text and appear in the individual chapter reference lists, however, they have been included here for the reader and researcher's convenience.

References

Baer, R.A., Smith, G.T., Hopkins, J., Krietemeyer, J., & Toney, L. (2006). Using self-report assessment methods to explore facets of mindfulness. *Assessment, 13*(1), 27–45.
Barbezat, D., & Bush, M. (2014). *Contemplative practices in higher education: Powerful methods to transform teaching and learning.* San Francisco: Jossey-Bass.
Bormann, J.E. (2010). Mantram repetition: A "portable contemplative practice" for modern times. In T.G. Plante (Ed.), *Contemplative practices in action: Spirituality, meditation, and health* (pp. 78–99). Santa Barbara: Praeger.
Brefczynski-Lewis, J.A., Lutz, A., Schaefer, H.S., Levinson, D.B., & Davidson, R.J. (2007). Neural correlates of attentional expertise in long-term meditation practitioners. *Proceedings of the National Academy of Sciences, 104*(27), 11483–11488. doi:10.1073/pnas.0606552104
Brown, K.W., & Ryan, R.M. (2003). The benefits of being present: Mindfulness and its role in psychological well-being. *Journal of Personality and Social Psychology, 84*(4), 822–848. doi:10.1037/0022-3514.84.doi:4.822
Cahn, B.R., & Polich, J. (2006). Meditation states and traits: EEG, ERP, and neuroimaging studies. *Psychological Bulletin, 132*(2), 180–211.
Cheever, N.A., Rosen, L.D., Carrier, L.M., & Chavez, A. (2014). Out of sight is not out of mind: The impact of restricting wireless mobile device use on anxiety levels among low, moderate and high users. *Computers in Human Behavior, 37,* 290–297. doi:10.1016/j.chb.2014.05.002

Chiesa, A., Calati, R., & Serretti, A. (2011). Does mindfulness training improve cognitive abilities? A systematic review of neuropsychological findings. *Clinical Psychology Review, 31*(3), 449–464. doi:10.1016/j.cpr.2010.11.003

Chiesa, A., & Malinowski, P. (2011). Mindfulness-based approaches: Are they all the same? *Journal of Clinical Psychology, 67*(4), 404–424. doi:10.1002/jclp.20776

Chiesa, A., & Serretti, A. (2009). Mindfulness-based stress reduction for stress management in healthy people: A review and meta-analysis. *The Journal of Alternative and Complementary Medicine, 15*(5), 593–600. doi:10.1089/acm.2008.0495

Colzato, L.S., Ozturk, A., & Hommel, B. (2012). Meditate to create: The impact of focused-attention and open-monitoring training on convergent and divergent thinking. *Frontiers in Psychology, 3*, 116. doi:10.3389/fpsyg.2012.00116

The Editors of *Time* (2016). *TIME mindfulness: The new science of health and happiness*. New York: Time Magazine.

Farias, M., & Wikholm, C. (2016). *The Buddha pill*. London: Watkins Media Limited.

Fox, K.C.R., Nijeboer, S., Dixon, M.L., Floman, J.L., Ellamil, M., Rumak, S.P., ... Christoff, K. (2014). Is meditation associated with altered brain structure? A systematic review and meta-analysis of morphometric neuroimaging in meditation practitioners. *Neuroscience & Biobehavioral Reviews, 43*, 48–73. doi:10.1016/j.neubiorev.2014.03.016

Gazzaley, A., & Rosen, L.D. (2016). *The distracted mind: Ancient brains in a high-tech world*. Cambridge, MA: MIT Press.

Gilpin, R. (2008). The use of Theravāda Buddhist practices and perspectives in mindfulness-based cognitive therapy. *Contemporary Buddhism, 9*(2), 227–251. doi:10.1080/14639940802556560

Goldberg, P. (2010). *American Veda: From Emerson and the Beatles to yoga and meditation: How Indian spirituality changed the West* (first edition). New York: Harmony Books.

Goleman, D. (1988). *The meditative mind: The varieties of meditative experience* (first edition). Los Angeles and New York: J.P. Tarcher.

Goleman, D., & Davidson, R.J. (2017). *Altered traits: Science reveals how meditation changes your mind, brain, and body*. New York: Avery.

Gollwitzer, P.M., & Sheeran, P. (2006). Implementation intentions and goal achievement: A meta-analysis of effects and processes. *Advances in Experimental Social Psychology, 38*, 69–119. doi:10.1016/S0065-2601(06)38002-38001

Gorman, T.E., & Green, C.S. (2016). Short-term mindfulness intervention reduces the negative attentional effects associated with heavy media multitasking. *Scientific Reports, 6*, 24542. doi:10.1038/srep24542. www.nature.com/articles/srep24542#supplementary-information.

Grossman, P., Niemann, L., Schmidt, S., & Walach, H. (2004). Mindfulness-based stress reduction and health benefits. *Journal of Psychosomatic Research, 57*(1), 35–43. doi:10.1016/S0022-3999(03)00573-7

Hutchison, M. (2003). *The book of floating: Exploring the private sea*. Nevada City: Gateway Books and Tapes.

Kabat-Zinn, J. (2005). *Coming to our senses: Healing ourselves and the world through mindfulness* (first edition). New York: Hyperion.

Kabat-Zinn, J. (2005). *Wherever you go, there you are: Mindfulness meditation in everyday life*. New York: Hyperion.

Kabat-Zinn, J. (2012). *Mindfulness for beginners: Reclaiming the present moment—and your life*. Boulder: Sounds True.

Kabat-Zinn, J. (2013). *Full catastrophe living: Using the wisdom of your body and mind to face stress, pain, and illness* (revised and updated edition). New York: Bantam Books.

Kapleau, P. (1966). *The three pillars of Zen: Teaching, practice, and enlightenment* (first US edition). New York: Harper & Row.

Kapleau, P. (1989). *Zen: Merging of East and West*. New York: Anchor Books.

Lepp, A., Barkley, J.E., & Karpinski, A.C. (2014). The relationship between cell phone use, academic performance, anxiety, and satisfaction with life in college students. *Computers in Human Behavior, 31*, 343–350.

Levy, D.M., Wobbrock, J.O., Kaszniak, A.W., & Ostergren, M. (2012). The effects of mindfulness meditation training on multitasking in a high-stress information environment. Paper presented at the Proceedings of Graphics Interface 2012, Toronto, Ontario, Canada.

Lilly, J.C. (2007). *The deep self: Consciousness exploration in the isolation tank*. Nevada City: Gateways Books and Tapes.

Lin, P., Chang, J., Zemon, V., & Midlarsky, E. (2007). Silent illumination: A study on Chan (Zen) meditation, anxiety, and musical performance quality. *Psychology of Music, 36*(2), 139–155. doi:10.1177/0305735607080840

Lippelt, D.P., Hommel, B., & Colzato, L.S. (2014). Focused attention, open monitoring and loving kindness meditation: Effects on attention, conflict monitoring, and creativity – a review. *Frontiers in Psychology, 5*(1083). doi:10.3389/fpsyg.2014.01083

Lutz, A., Slagter, H.A., Dunne, J.D., & Davidson, R.J. (2008). Attention regulation and monitoring in meditation. *Trends in Cognitive Sciences, 12*(4), 163–169. doi:10.1016/j.tics.2008.01.00doi:5

MacLean, K.A., Ferrer, E., Aichele, S.R., Bridwell, D.A., Zanesco, A.P., Jacobs, T.L., … Saron, C.D. (2010). Intensive meditation training improves perceptual discrimination and sustained attention. *Psychological Science, 20*(10), 1–11.

McCown, D., Reibel, D., & Micozzi, M.S. (2010). *Teaching mindfulness: A practical guide for clinicians and educators*. New York and London: Springer.

Minear, M., Brasher, F., McCurdy, M., Lewis, J., & Younggren, A. (2013). Working memory, fluid intelligence, and impulsiveness in heavy media multitaskers. *Psychonomic Bulletin & Review, 20*(6), 1274–1281.

Mrazek, M.D., Franklin, M.S., Phillips, D.T., Baird, B., & Schooler, J.W. (2013). Mindfulness training improves working memory capacity and GRE performance while reducing mind wandering. *Psychological Science, 241*(5), 776–781.

Mrazek, M.D., Smallwood, J., & Schooler, J.W. (2012). Mindfulness and mind-wandering: Finding convergence through opposing constructs. *Emotion, 12*(3), 442–448.

Murphy, M., Donovan, S., & Taylor, E. (1997). *The physical and psychological effects of meditation: A review of contemporary research with a comprehensive bibliography, 1931–1996* (second edition). Sausalito: Institute of Noetic Sciences.

Neff, K.D., & Pommier, E. (2013). The relationship between self-compassion and other-focused concern among college undergraduates, community adults, and practicing meditators. *Self and Identity, 12*(2), 160–176. doi:10.1080/15298868.2011.649546

Ophira, E., Nassb, C., & Wagner, A.D. (2009). Cognitive control in media multitaskers. *Proceedings of the National Academy of Sciences, 106*(37), 15583–15587.

Plante, T.G. (2010). *Contemplative practices in action: Spirituality, meditation, and health*. Santa Barbara: Praeger.

Ragoonaden, K. (2015). *Mindful teaching and learning: Developing a pedagogy of well-being*. Lanham: Lexington Books.

Ralph, B.C.W., Thomson, D.R., Cheyne, J.A., & Smilek, D. (2014). Media multitasking and failures of attention in everyday life. *Psychological Research*, 78(5), 661–669.

Rapgay, L., & Bystrisky, A. (2009). Classical mindfulness. *Annals of the New York Academy of Sciences*, 1172(1), 148–162. doi:10.1111/j.1749-6632.2009.04405.x

Rogers, H. (2016). *The mindful twenty-something: Life skills to handle stress … and everything else*. Oakland: New Harbinger Publications.

Rojiani, R., Santoyo, J.F., Rahrig, H., Roth, H.D., & Britton, W.B. (2017). Women benefit more than men in response to college-based meditation training. *Frontiers in Psychology*, 8, 551. doi:10.3389/fpsyg.2017.00551

Satchidananda, S.S. (2012). *The Yoga Sutras of Patanjali*. United States: Integral Yoga Publications.

Schonert-Reichl, K. (2016). *Handbook of mindfulness in education: Integrating theory and research into practice*. New York: Springer.

Sedlmeier, P., Eberth, J., Schwarz, M., Zimmermann, D., Haarig, F., Jaeger, S., & Kunze, S. (2012). The psychological effects of meditation: A meta-analysis. *Psychological Bulletin*, 138(6), 1139–1171. doi:10.1037/a0028168

Segal, Z.V., Williams, J.M.G., & Teasdale, J.D. (2002). *Mindfulness-based cognitive therapy for depression: A new approach to preventing relapse*. New York: Guilford Press.

Shapiro, D.H., & Walsh, R.N. (1984). *Meditation, classic and contemporary perspectives*. New York: Aldine Pub. Co.

Shy, Y. (2017). *What now? Meditation for your twenties and beyond*. Berkeley: Parallax Press.

Slagter, H.A., Lutz, A., Greischar, L.L., Francis, A.D., Nieuwenhuis, S., Davis, J.M., & Davidson, R.J. (2007). Mental training affects distribution of limited brain resources. *PLOS Biology*, 5(6), e138. doi:10.1371/journal.pbio.0050138

Sriwilai, K., & Charoensukmongkol, P. (2015). Face it, don't Facebook it: Impacts of social media addiction on mindfulness, coping strategies and the consequence on emotional exhaustion. *Stress and Health*, 32, 427–434.

Tang, Y.-Y., Holzel, B.K., & Posner, M.I. (2015). The neuroscience of mindfulness meditation. *Nat Rev Neurosci*, 16(4), 213–225. doi:10.1038/nrn3916

Tart, C.T. (1969). *Altered states of consciousness: A book of readings*. New York: Wiley.

Tart, C.T. (1971). A psychologist's experience with transcendental meditation. *Journal of Transpersonal Psychology*, 3(1), 135–140.

Timmons, B., & Kamiya, J. (1970). The psychology and physiology of meditation and related phenomena: A bibliography. *Journal of Transpersonal Psychology*, 2(1), 41–59.

Valentine, E.R., & Sweet, P.L.G. (1999). Meditation and attention: A comparison of the effects of concentrative and mindfulness meditation on sustained attention. *Mental Health, Religion & Culture*, 2(1), 59–70. doi:10.1080/13674679908406332

Wachholtz, A.B., & Pargament, K.I. (2005). Is spirituality a critical ingredient of meditation? Comparing the effects of spiritual meditation, secular meditation, and relaxation on spiritual, psychological, cardiac, and pain outcomes. *Journal of Behavioral Medicine*, 28(4), 369–384. doi:10.1007/s10865-005-9008-5

Wallace, B.A. (2006). *The attention revolution: Unlocking the power of the focused mind* (first Wisdom edition). Boston: Wisdom Publications.

Wallace, B.A., & Bodhi, V.B. (2006). The nature of mindfulness and its role in Buddhist meditation: A correspondence between B. Allan Wallace and the Venerable Bhikkhu Bodhi. *Clinical Psychology Science & Practice* (Winter). Retrieved from http://shamatha.org/sites/default/files/Bhikkhu_Bodhi_Correspondence.pdf.

Watts, A. (1957). *The way of Zen*. New York: Pantheon.

Watts, A. (1960). *This is it, and other essays on Zen and spiritual experience*. New York: Pantheon Books.

Wilber, K. (1999). *Integral psychology: Transformations of consciousness, selected essays* (first edition). Boston: Shambhala.

Wilber, K. (1999). *The spectrum of consciousness: No boundary, selected essays* (first edition). Boston: Shambhala.

Wilber, K. (2016). *Integral meditation: Mindfulness as a way to grow up, wake up, and show up in your life* (first edition). Boulder: Shambhala.

Wilber, K., Engler, J., & Brown, D.P. (1986). *Transformations of consciousness: conventional and contemplative perspectives on development* (first edition). Boston and New York: New Science Library.

Zanesco, A.P., King, B.G., MacLean, K.A., & Saron, C.D. (2013). Executive control and felt concentrative engagement following intensive meditation training. *Frontiers in Human Neuroscience*, 7, 566. doi:10.3389/fnhum.2013.00566

APPENDIX C

Organizations, Programs, and Apps

In the following list, you will find a number of groups, organizations, and websites that predominately support meditation training and education in schools or other institutions as well as support services for individuals and educators. Some of these groups will be more appropriate for educators in an institutional setting (such as a university) than the individual. Also, some of these organizations have membership fees or dues. So, please use discretion in deciding which groups or organizations are appropriate and valuable in your particular situation.

Groups and Organizations

The American Mindfulness Research Association (AMRA) was founded in 2013. Its mission is to support empirical and conceptual efforts to: (1) establish an evidence base for the process, practice, and construct of mindfulness; (2) promote best evidence-based standards for the use of mindfulness research and its applications; and (3) facilitate discovery and professional development through grant-giving.

AMRA serves as a professional resource to the sciences and humanities, practice communities, and the broader public on mindfulness from the perspective of contemplative practice.

AMRA is a membership organization with an annual dues structure. Membership gains you access to an extensive list of research articles (updated regularly).

It also maintains a contact list of mindfulness-based research and training programs.

AMRA website: https://goamra.org/

The Association for Contemplative Mind in Higher Education (ACMHE) is a multidisciplinary academic association with an international membership of educators, administrators, staff, students, researchers, and other professionals committed to the transformation of higher education through the recovery and development of the contemplative dimensions of teaching, learning, and knowing.

The ACMHE promotes the emergence of a broad culture of contemplation in the academy, connects a broad network of academic professionals with online resources, and stimulates scholarship and research concerning contemplative pedagogy, methodology, and epistemology within and across disciplines through initiatives and events including the annual ACMHE national conference.

The ACMHE is an initiative of the Center for Contemplative Mind in Society (CMind), a non-profit organization described below that works to integrate contemplative awareness and contemporary life in order to create a more just, compassionate, reflective, and sustainable society. For almost 20 years, CMind has fostered the inclusion of contemplative practice and inquiry in colleges and universities.

ACMHE website: www.contemplativemind.org/programs/acmhe

The Center for Contemplative Mind in Society (CMind) is a 501-c(3) non-profit organization based in Northampton, Massachusetts. It works to transform higher education by supporting and encouraging the use of contemplative/introspective practices and perspectives to create active learning and research environments that look deeply into experience and meaning for all in service of a more just and compassionate society.

The Center for Contemplative Mind in Society website: www.contemplativemind.org

The Center for Mindfulness & Human Potential (CMHP) is a recently established UC Santa Barbara research center which is dedicated to advancing interdisciplinary research into mindfulness and neuroplasticity. The center—which is directed by long-standing collaborators Jonathan Schooler, Michael Mrazek, and Dawa Tarchin Phillips—aims to use the best science, education and technology to advance scientific understanding and improve lives.

CMHP website: www.cmhp.ucsb.edu/

The Center for Mindfulness in Medicine, Healthcare, and Society is a part of the University of Massachusetts Medical School and is the program co-founded by Jon Kabat-Zinn to disseminate Mindfulness-Based Stress Reduction Therapy (MBSR). The Center's website is a robust information source about mindfulness (particularly MBSR training). In addition to offering professional training in MBSR, it also maintains a list of retreat centers that host multi-day silent retreats at this address: www.umassmed.edu/cfm/training/retreats/.

Center for Mindfulness website: www.umassmed.edu/cfm/

Mindful Schools is an organization that offers educators (primarily K-12) practical skills for self-care, facilitation, and connecting with youth, providing simple, effective mindfulness practices that can be integrated into the school day and adapted for diverse environments.

Mindful Schools website: www.mindfulschools.org

The Mindful Awareness Research Center (MARC) is a partner of the Norman Cousins Center for Psychoneuroimmunology within the Jane and Terry Semel Institute for Neuroscience and Human Behavior at UCLA. MARC's mission is to foster mindful awareness across the lifespan through education and research to promote well-being and a more compassionate society.

MARC website: www.marc.ucla.edu

The University of California–San Diego Center for Mindfulness is a multi-faceted program of professional training, education, research and outreach intended to further the practice and integration of mindfulness into all aspects of society. Much like the Center for Mindfulness in Medicine, Healthcare, and Society described above, it offers professional MBSR teacher training and certification.

UC San Diego Center for Mindfulness website: https://health.ucsd.edu/specialties/mindfulness/Pages/default.aspx

Programs and Centers

Following is a list of more than 50 primarily university medical school-sponsored mindfulness programs and research centers that offer various forms of mindfulness-based training to their patients, medical students, staff, and general public.

Buchanan Counseling Center, Indiana University School of Medicine, 1812 N Capitol Ave, Indianapolis, IN 46202, http://iuhealth.org/methodist/behavioral-health/buchanan-counseling-center

Center for Compassion and Altruism Research and Education (CCARE), Stanford University School of Medicine, 1070 Arastradero Road, Palo Alto, CA 94304, http://ccare.stanford.edu

Center for Exploring Mind-Body Interactions, University of Utah School of Medicine, 615 Arapeen Drive, Salt Lake City, UT 84108, http://painresearch.utah.edu

Center for Health and Wellbeing, University of Vermont College of Medicine, 146 South Williams Street, Burlington, VT 05401, www.uvm.edu/~chwb/psych/?Page=mindfulness.html&SM=mindfulnessmenu.html

Center for Integrated Health, Vanderbilt University School of Medicine, 1211 Medical Center Drive, Nashville, TN 37232, www.vanderbilthealth.com/integrativehealth

Center for Integrated Medicine, George Washington University, 908 New Hampshire Ave NW, Washington, DC, DC 20037, www.gwcim.com/about

Center of Integrative Health, University of Florida College of Medicine, 2000 Southwest Archer Road, Gainesville, FL 32608, https://ufhealth.org/integrative-medicine/about-us

Center for Integrative Health and Wellness, Ohio State University College of Medicine, 1581 Dodd Dr, Columbus, OH 43210, http://medicalcenter.osu.edu/patientcare/healthcare_services/integrative_medicine/pages/index.aspx

Center for Integrative Health and Wellness, University of Cincinnati College of Medicine, 2220 Victory Parkway, Cincinnati, OH, http://med.uc.edu/integrative

Center for Integrative Medicine, University of California, Irvine, School of Medicine, 1202 Bristol Street, Costa Mesa, CA 92626, www.sscim.uci.edu/mindfulness-programs.asp

Center for Integrative Medicine, University of Maryland School of Medicine, 2200 Kernan Drive, Baltimore, MD 21207, www.compmed.umm.edu/default.asp

Center for Integrative Medicine, University of Pittsburgh School of Medicine, 580 S Aiken Ave, Pittsburgh, PA 15232, www.upmc.com/Services/integrative-medicine/Pages/default.aspx

Center for Integrative Medicine, Stanford University School of Medicine, 211 Quarry Road, Palo Alto, CA 94304, http://stanfordhealthcare.org/medical-clinics/integrative-medicine-center.html

Center for Investigating Healthy Minds, Waisman Center, University of Wisconsin School of Medicine and Public Health, 500 Highland Avenue, Madison, WI 53705, www.investigatinghealthyminds.org

Center for Life, University of New Mexico School of Medicine, 4700 Jefferson Street Northeast, Albuquerque, NM 87109, http://unmmg.org/clinics/cfl/index.html

Center for Mind and Brain, University of California, Davis, School of Medicine, 267 Cousteau Place, Davis, CA 95618, http://mindbrain.ucdavis.edu

Center for Mindfulness and Compassion, Cambridge Health Alliance, Harvard Medical School, 26 Central Street, Somerville, MA 02143, www.chacmc.org

Center for Mindfulness at UC San Diego Health Systems, University of California, San Diego, 5060 Shoreham Place, San Diego, CA, http://health.ucsd.edu/specialties/mindfulness/Pages/default.aspx

Centre for Mindfulness Research and Practice, Bangor University, Bangor, Gwynedd, LL57 2DG, www.bangor.ac.uk/mindfulness

Centro de Pratica e Estudo de Mindfulness, Universidade de Aveiro 3810–193 Aveiro, Portugal, http://mindfulness.web.ua.pt

City University London, Centre for Psychological Wellbeing and Neuroscience, Whiskin Street, London, EC1R 0JD, http://www.city.ac.uk/arts-social-sciences/psychology/research/centre-for-psychological-well-being-and-neuroscience

Complementary and Integrative Medicine Program, Mayo Medical School, 200 1st Street Southwest, Rochester, MN 55905, www.mayoclinic.org/departments-centers/general-internal-medicine/minnesota/overview/specialty-groups/complementary-integrative-medicine

Danish Center for Mindfulness, Department of Clinical Medicine, Aarhus University Hospital, Barthsgade 5, 8200 Aarhus N, Denmark, http://mindfulness.au.dk/en

Duke Integrative Medicine, Duke University, 3475 Erwin Road, Durham, NC 27705, www.dukeintegrativemedicine.org

Institute for Mindfulness, Switzerland, Müliwiesstrasse 55, 8487 Zell, Switzerland, http://instituteformindfulness.org

Integrative Health Center, University of Arizona College of Medicine, 3033 North Central Avenue, Phoenix, Arizona, https://ihc.arizona.edu

Integrative Medicine Center, MD Anderson Cancer Center, University of Texas Medical School at Houston, 1515 Holcombe Blvd, Houston, Texas 77030, www.mdanderson.org/patient-and-cancer-information/care-centers-and-clinics/specialty-and-treatment-centers/integrative-medicine-center/index.html

Integrative Medicine Program, University of Wisconsin School of Medicine and Public Health, 621 Science Dr, Madison, WI 53711, www.fammed.wisc.edu/integrative

Lotus Meditation Center, University of North Dakota School of Medicine and Health Sciences, 2908 University Ave, Grand Forks, ND 58202, http://und.edu/lotus-center

Mindful Awareness Research Center (MARC), University of California, Los Angeles, School of Medicine, 760 Westwood Plaza, Los Angeles, CA, http://marc.ucla.edu/

Mindful Living Lab, Catholic University of America, 620 Michigan Ave NE, Washington, DC 20064, https://sites.google.com/site/cuamindfullivinglab/home

Mindful Medicine at Integrative Pain Care, 437 Remuera Road, Remuera, Auckland 1050, New Zealand, www.drnickpenney.com

Mindful USC, University of Southern California, Los Angeles, CA 90089, http://mindful.usc.edu

Mindfulness Center, Georgetown University School of Medicine, 4963 Elm St., Suite 100 Bethesda, MD 20814, www.themindfulnesscenter.org

Mindfulness Clinic, University of Utah Counseling Services, University of Utah School of Medicine, 201 South 1460 East, Salt Lake City, UT 84112, http://counselingcenter.utah.edu/services/mindfulness.php

Mindfulness and Education Working Group, Columbia University Teachers College, 525 West 120th Street, New York 10027, www.tc.columbia.edu/centers/mindfulness

Mindfulness Institute, Jefferson Medical College of Thomas Jefferson University, 1015 Chestnut Street, Philadelphia, PA 19107, http://hospitals.jefferson.edu/departments-and-services/mindfulness-institute

Mindfulness Practice Center, University of Missouri-Columbia School of Medicine, One Hospital Dr, Columbia, MO 65212, www.umsystem.edu/curators/mindfulness

Mindfulness Programs at University of Iowa Hospitals and Clinics, University of Iowa College of Medicine, 200 Hawkins Drive, Iowa City, IA 52242, www.uihealthcare.org/mindfulness/

Mindfulness Research and Practice Initiative, University of Miami School of Medicine, 1251 Stanford Drive, Coral Gables, FL 33146, http://mindfulness.miami.edu/index.html

Mindfulness, Stress & Health Lab, University of Pennsylvania, Perelman School of Medicine, 3535 Market Street, Suite 670, Philadelphia, 19104, www.mindfulnesslab.org

Oregon Center for Complementary and Alternative Medicine in Neurological Disorders, Oregon Health & Science University School of Medicine, 3181 Southwest Sam

Jackson Park Road, Portland, OR 97239, www.ohsu.edu/xd/research/centers-institutes/neurology/orccamind

Osher Center for Integrative Medicine, University of California, San Francisco, School of Medicine, 1545 Divisadero Street, San Francisco, CA, United States, www.osher.ucsf.edu

Oxford Mindfulness Centre, Oxford University, Oxford, OX3 7JX, United Kingdom, http://oxfordmindfulness.org

Penn Program for Mindfulness, University of Pennsylvania School of Medicine, 3930 Chestnut Street, 4th Floor Philadelphia, PA 19104, www.pennmedicine.org/mindfulness

Program on Integrative Medicine, University of North Carolina at Chapel Hill School of Medicine, 321 S Columbia St, Chapel Hill, NC, United States, www.med.unc.edu/phyrehab/pim

Studies in Mindfulness, University of Aberdeen, Elphinstone Road, Aberdeen, AB24 3TU, www.abdn.ac.uk/study/courses/postgraduate/taught/studies_in_mindfulness

Syracuse University Mind Body Laboratory, 430 Huntington Hall Syracuse, NY 13204, http://mindbodylab.syr.edu

Tom Baker Cancer Centre Mindfulness Based Cancer Recovery Program, 2202 2nd St. SW Calgary, Alberta, Canada, http://tbccintegrative.com

UVA Mindfulness Center, University of Virginia School of Medicine, 21 University Circle, Charlottesville, VA 22903, www.medicine.virginia.edu/clinical/departments/medicine/divisions/general-med/wellness/the-mindfulness-center/home.html

Wellness & Chronic Illness Program, Stony Brook University School of Medicine, 2500 Nesconset Hwy, Stony Brook, NY 11790, www.stonybrookmedicalcenter.org/wellness

Apps

While these (and others) were examined earlier in the book, these brief profiles are included here for the convenience of the reader.

Headspace is a digital service that provides guided meditation sessions and mindfulness training. Its content can be accessed online or via its mobile apps. In April 2016, Headspace claimed to have over six million people using its programs.

Headspace was founded in 2010 by Andy Puddicombe, a former Buddhist monk, and Rich Pierson, a marketing and brand development executive. To date, the company has raised over $30 million dollars and its training app is considered one of the most successful apps in the mindfulness space.

Website: www.headspace.com

Calm is another highly popular meditation instruction app. It is both similar to and different from Headspace. Calm uses a female narrator with a cheery, enthusiastic voice. The "basics" Calm series, very much like that of Headspace, is a seven-day progression, starting with a three-minute session and working up to a 12-minute session on day seven. At this point, you are encouraged to join the subscription model by, once again, inputting your credit card for monthly or annual charging cycles.

Website: www.calm.com/

Muse is a $299 biofeedback device that measures brainwave activity through a fitted plastic headband embedded with seven electroencephalography (EEG) sensors that monitor your brain and transmit that data, using Bluetooth radio waves, to an app on your smartphone. The app then gives you feedback using soundscapes and imagery on your phone to help you target and identify "states of relaxation." The theory is that wearing the device while meditating can help "guide" you toward deeper, more relaxing meditative states.

In practice, the Muse headset is simple to use and the app has an orientation session that helps you calibrate the device to your body each time it runs. Muse offers a series of guided meditations, some of which are led by well-known personalities like Deepak Chopra, and a series of "soundscapes" that adapt to the data your brainwaves provide.

Website: www.choosemuse.com/

INDEX

active/hyperactive thinking 48–49, 100, 114
actors, training of x–xi
Advanced Consciousness Training (A.C.T.) for Actors (Page) 2, 40
Alpert, Richard. *See* Ram Dass
Altered States (Chayefsky) 77
Altered States of Consciousness (Tart) 7
American College Health Association (ACHA) 8
American College of Sports Medicine 64
American Mindfulness Research Association (AMRA) 89–90, 136
American Psychological Association (APA) 63
anxiety 8–10, 77; social 9, 23, 35, 53, 119
apps and devices xvi, 97, 111, 141–42; Calm xvi, 141–42; Koru 39, 40; Mindful USC 85; Muse (wearable EEG monitor) xvi, 74–75, 142; virtual reality platforms 74
Arnett, Jeffery 9
Association for Contemplative Mind in Higher Education (ACMHE) 88–89, 136–37
attention 1, 2, 4–6, 113; bare 4, 6, 61, 76
attentional shifting 36
attention span xv, 22–26
audio recordings 34, 73, 76–77, 82, 84
The Autobiography of a Yogi (Yogananda) 6
awareness training x–xi

BaDuanJin Qigong 10–11
Baime, Michael 86
bare attention 4, 6, 61, 76
basic mindfulness practice xiv, xvii, 96–98
bathing, mindful xvi, 51–52, 103
beginner's mind 5
Be Here Now (Ram Dass) 7
belly breathing 39
Binaural Beats xvi, 75–77
body scan 56; breath and 16–18; Koru 39; traditional 15–20, 30, 99–100, 112, 113
boredom 64–65
brainwave entrainment technology xvi, 73, 75–77
brain wave frequencies 75
breath xv, 3, 56–57; belly breathing 39; chicken breath 39; conscious breathing 10–15, 57, 99–100, 112, 113; counting or labeling xv, 30, 113–14; diaphragmatic breathing 39; FAM on the breath xv, 27–30, 57, 101–2, 113–14, 115; traditional body scan and 16–18
breath-cycle 27–30
Buddhist tradition 7, 33, 81

Calm (mobile app) xvi, 141–42
Canadian research 23–24
Casta, Aurora 107
Center for Collegiate Mental Health (CCMH) 8–10

144 Index

Center for Contemplative Mind in Society (CMind) 88–89, 137
Center for Koru Mindfulness 38
Center for Mindfulness (CFM) Certified MBSR Teacher 35; list of retreat facilities 97–98
Center for Mindfulness & Human Potential (CMHP) 137
Center for Mindfulness in Medicine, Health Care, and Society (University of Massachusetts Medical School) 35, 80, 137, 138
check-in activities 39, 65
chicken breath 39
choiceless awareness 36
Chopra, Deepak 75, 142
clocks 2
clothing, comfortable 11
Cognitive Control in Media Multitaskers (Ophira et al.) 22–23, 24
College Mindfulness Training (CMT) xvi; basic parameters of course 110–19; course policies and expectations 122–23; developing institutional program 106; generic course syllabus 107; goal and intention setting 108–9; grading 112, 123; individual and collective approaches 94–95; length of meditation sessions 41, 54; one-semester course xvii, 40–41, 111–19; outside of academic environment 41; progressive and cumulative 48–49; silent retreat 41, 123–24; tentative class schedule 123–30. *See also* individual practice
College Mindfulness Training (Page) 41, 122
concentration meditation 5. *See also* Focused Attention Meditation (FAM)
conscious breathing 10–15, 57, 99–100, 112, 113
consciousness, states of xv, 1, 49, 80
"cosmic consciousness" 66
counseling services 8–10, 23, 37–38, 107, 120
credit-bearing courses xii–xiv, xvii, 40–41, 83, 91, 95, 106. *See also* College Mindfulness Training (CMT); syllabus
cultural movement, mindfulness as xii–xiii, 1, 6–8, 80
cultural revolution of the 1960s 6

database on mindfulness 90
depression 8–10, 23
developmental stages 9
dharma 33, 34
diaphragmatic breathing 39
digital age, postmodern 22
digital distraction 22, 52, 73–74, 100–101
The Distracted Mind (Gazzaley and Rosen) 25–26
distraction 118; apps and 73–74; digital 22, 52, 73–74, 100–101; Koru techniques for 39
Duke University Student Counseling Center 37

eating xvi, 2–3, 39; in medical MBSR setting 36; Mindful Eating Exercise #1 3–4, 98–99, 111; Mindful Eating Exercise #2 xvi, 49–51, 103, 115; raisin-eating exercise 3
EEG monitors xvi, 73, 74–75, 142
emerging adults, college-aged xi–xvi, 112; mind/body fitness and 63–72, 84; stress and 8–10, 36; work, love, and worldviews 9
Emerson Elementary School (Oakland, CA) 90
emotion-focused coping 24
emotions and memories 2, 4, 36
everyday life 48–62; bathing 51–52; eating 49–51; mini-retreat 54–57; OMM or mindfulness meditation practice 57–61; technology, mindfulness of 52–54, 99–100, 115
evidence-based skills 37
exercise, nutrition, and fitness training xvi, 84
Exercise for Mood and Anxiety: Proven Strategies for Overcoming Depression and Enhancing Well-Being (Otto and Smits) 64
exercises, experiential xiv, xv; conscious breathing 10–15, 57, 99–100, 112, 113; FAM on the breath xv, 27–30, 57, 101–2, 113–14, 115; four-hour silent mini-retreat xvi, 56–57; mantra-walking/jogging exercise xvi, 69–70, 102, 104; mindful bathing xvi, 51–52, 103; Mindful Eating Exercise #1 3–4, 48, 98–99, 111; Mindful Eating Exercise #2 xvi, 49–51, 103, 115; mindful movement exercise 41–45; seated mantra meditation xvi, 66–67, 104; traditional body scan 15–20, 30, 99–100, 112, 113; watch exercise 2, 4, 98–99, 111

eye contact 55, 56
eyes, soft focus 16, 20, 28, 58–59, 66

Facebook 22
flotation therapy xvi, 77–78
Focused Attention Meditation (FAM) 5, 65, 80, 111; counting or labeling variation xv, 30, 113–14; FAM on the breath xv, 27–30, 57, 101–2, 113–14, 115; mindful movement—walking xvi, 69–70, 102, 103, 114, 115; traditional body scan 15–20, 30, 99–100, 112, 113. *See also* mantra
formal meditation practice 48
Four Hour Silent Mini-Retreat xvi
Full Catastrophe Living: Using the Wisdom of Your Body and Mind to Face Stress, Pain, and Illness (Kabat-Zinn) 34

gathas (meditation poems) 39
Gazzaley, Adam 25–26
Global Spiritual Life Center 81
goal and intention setting xvii, 51, 95–96, 108–9; contingency 96; meta-goals 96, 110
Gollwitzer, P. M. 96, 109
grading 112, 123
Graduate Records Exam (GRE) 10
Guiding Teachers 91

habituation 66
Headspace (mobile app) xvi, 141
Hinduism 65–66
HMMs (heavy media multitaskers) 23–25
home-study courses 84

imagery 11, 37, 39, 74
implementation intentions 96, 109
individual practice 94–105; basic parameters 96–98; goal and intention setting 95–96; length of time 97; OMM 103–4; retreats 97, 103, 104; sample program 98–105
industry, mindfulness as xii, xvii, 1, 80
informal mindfulness practice xvi, 39–40, 48, 54
information foragers 26
institutional settings xvi–xvii, 26–27, 106; CMT instructor's personal practice 107–8; what is CMT practice 108. *See also* programs and initiatives
instructors: basic programmatic requirements xvii; CMT instructor's personal practice xvii, 107–8; goal and intention setting xvii; personal experience xiv–xv; teacher certification x–xii, 32, 35, 84–86, 90–93, 97–98, 107
Integral Meditation: Mindfulness as a Way to Grow Up, Wake Up, and Show Up in Your Life (Wilber) 115, 122
internal events 2, 77
internally guided exercise 20
iPhone 22

Jane and Terry Semel Institute for Neuroscience and Human Behavior 138
journaling 39, 40, 110, 112–13, 115, 116
Journal of Contemplative Inquiry 89

K-12 educators 90–93
Kabat-Zinn, Jon x, xii, 1, 4, 7, 32–35, 84
Kent State University 24
Koru Mindfulness Program xv, 10, 36, 37–40, 107; app 39, 40; check-in process 39; four-week sequence 38–40; Koru 2.0 40; length of meditation sessions 38, 40, 54; meditation logs 39

labeling: breaths xv, 30, 113–14; of feelings 40; of thoughts 39, 60
length of meditation sessions 36, 38, 40, 41, 54
letting go 39, 60
Lilly, John C. 77
LMMs (light media multitaskers) 23–25
Lock, Edwin A. 95–96, 109
loosening of consciousness 49

Maharishi Mahesh Yogi 65
mantra xvi, 5, 116–17; as point of focus 65–66; seated meditation xvi, 66–67, 104; selecting 66. *See also* Focused Attention Meditation (FAM)
Ma-ori people 37
Maytan, Margaret 36, 37, 40
MBSR Program. *See* Mindfulness-Based Stress Reduction
McGill University experiments 77
media multi-tasking 22
medical uses of meditation 7, 10, 32, 35–36, 86
meditation: benefits 25, 65, 86–87, 94, 102, 104–5, 108, 119; forms 6; mindfulness as type of 1, 4–6, 80; non-judgmental state 1, 2, 5, 6; predictable path of 48–49; secularized practice x, xv–xvi, 7, 33
"meditation environments" 74

meditation upon conscious experience 5. *See also* Open Monitoring Meditation (OMM)
mental health 8–9; discontinuing CMT 116; exercises and 63. *See also* stress
mind/body fitness 63–72, 84; mindful exercise 64–65; self-care 63–64
mind/body or integrative medicine 32
Mindful Awareness Research Center (MARC) 138
Mindful Educator Essentials course 91–92
mindful movement practices 41–45, 84
mindful movement—walking xvi, 69–70, 102, 103, 114, 115
mindfulness: as catch-all term xi; as cultural movement xii–xiii, 1, 6–8, 80; definitions 1, 80, 94, 108; as industry xii, xvii, 1, 80; primary areas of impact 27; as state of individual consciousness 1, 2–4; of technology 52–54, 99–100, 115; as type of meditation practice 1, 4–6, 80
Mindfulness-Based Cognitive Therapy (MBCT) 10, 84
mindfulness-based interventions (MBIs) 8
Mindfulness-Based Stress Management 86–88
Mindfulness-Based Stress Reduction (MBSR) xv, 1, 7, 10, 32–47; eight-week course x, 35–36; full-day retreat 36; homework 36; length of meditation sessions 36, 54; pre-screening 35; rules and expectations 36; silent retreats 36; sources 34; teacher certification x–xii, 32, 84–85, 107
Mindfulness for the Next Generation: Helping Emerging Adults Manage Stress and Lead Healthier Lives (Rogers and Maytan) 38
Mindfulness Fundamentals course 91
Mindfulness Research Monthly 90
Mindfulness Training Improves Working Memory: Capacity and GRE Performance while Reducing Mind Wandering (Mrazek et al.) 10
MindfulNYU 81–83
Mindful Schools 90–93, 137
Mindful Self-Compassion 84
Mindful Teacher Year-Long Certification Program 92
The Mindful Twenty-Something: Life Skills to Handle Stress & Everything Else (Rogers) 38
mini-retreat 54–57, 78, 117
monkey mind xvi, 48

mPEAK Training 84
Mrazek, Michael 137
multi-tasking xv, xvi, 22, 52, 100–101; Michigan State University research 23; Stanford University research 22–23; Taiwanese research 24; University of Wisconsin-Madison research 25
Muse (wearable EEG monitor) xvi, 74–75, 142

New Age spirituality 6
New York University 81–83
non-attachment 60
non-judgmental state 1, 2, 5, 6, 16, 49, 100, 114
non-students xiii–xiv
Norman Cousins Center for Psychoneuroimmunology 138

on-task and off-task thoughts 23
Open Monitoring Meditation (OMM) xv, xvi, 5–6, 36, 57–61, 65, 80, 111, 115; choiceless awareness 36; individual practice 103–4
organizations xvi–xvii, 136–38
Otto, Michael 64

Penn Program for Mindfulness 86–88
Phillips, Dawa Tarchin 137
physical exercise/fitness analogy 94–95, 108
Pierson, Rich 141
present moment 1, 2–3
programs and initiatives xvi–xvii, 26–27, 80–93, 138–41; Center for Contemplative Mind in Society (CMind) 88–89; MindfulNYU 81–83; Mindful Schools 90–93; Mindful USC 85–86; Penn Program for Mindfulness 86–88; University of California—San Diego Center for Mindfulness 83–85. *See also* institutional settings
Puddicombe, Andy 141
puppy dog mind 6, 48

Qigong 10–11

raisin-eating exercise 3
Ram Dass 7
randomized controlled trials 25, 40
readings and research 102, 115, 122, 131–35

recordings, guided meditation xv, 84, 85, 97, 111, 112
relational disruption 22
Relationship Between Cell Phone Use, Academic Performance, Anxiety, and Satisfaction with Life in College Students (Kent State University) 24
restricted environmental stimulation therapy (REST) 78
retreats, mindfulness 97. *See also* silent meditation retreats
Rogers, Holly 10, 36, 37–40, 107
Rosen, Larry D. 25–26

Sanskrit 66
Schooler, Jonathan 137
seated mantra meditation xvi, 66–67, 104
secularized meditation practice x, xv–xvi, 7, 33
self-awareness x–xi, 32
self-care practice xiii–xiv, xvi, 63–64
self-regulatory behaviors 96, 109–10
self-training 40
sensations, awareness of x–xi. *See also* body scan
sensory deprivation techniques xvi, 77–78
Sheeran, P. 96, 109
Shibashi 10
Shurley, Jay T. 77
Shy, Yael 81–83
Siddhartha (The Buddha) 66
silent meditation retreats xi, xvi, 36, 41, 117, 123–24; mini-retreat 54–57, 78, 117; secure space 55; UCSD Center for Mindfulness 84
sleep during meditation exercises 15, 20, 28, 99
smell, sense of 50, 52, 59–60
Smits, Jasper 64
social anxiety 9, 23, 35, 53, 119
social interaction 53, 55, 56
sounds, sense of 6, 20, 50, 51–52, 60
soundscapes 75
space and equipment 96–97, 110

stress: adult population xi; in emerging adulthood 8–10, 36; reduction techniques 10, 34
Stress-Out Kids: Mindfulness for Tweens and Teens 87
stress reaction profile 9
"subtle energies" 11
Summer Session on Contemplative Pedagogy 89
syllabus xvii, 120–30; purpose of course and learning goals 121–22; recommended texts 122

T'ai Chi Ch'uan 10
talking stick 117
Tart, Charles C. 7
task-switching exercises 23
teacher training programs 84–86; Mindful Schools 90–93
technology: apps and devices xvi, 39, 40; brainwave entrainment technology xvi, 73, 75–77; exercise and 64; mantras and 68–69; mindfulness of 52–54, 99–100, 115; phones 22
Tibet 6–7
Time magazine 8
timers 74, 97, 110
Toward the Integration of Meditation into Higher Education (Shapiro et al.) 27
traditional body scan 15–20, 30, 99–100, 112, 113
Transcendental Meditation (TM) 7, 65–66

University of California—San Diego (UCSD) Center for Mindfulness 83–85, 107, 138
University of Massachusetts Medical Center Hospital 7, 32–35, 80, 137
University of Pennsylvania 86, 107
University of Southern California (USC) 85–86

Vedas 66
virtual reality platforms 74

walking meditation xvi, 39, 41–45, 56; mantra-walking/jogging exercise xvi, 69–70, 102, 104; mindful movement—walking xvi, 69–70, 102, 103, 114, 115
watch exercise 2, 4, 98–99, 111
water-tank systems 77

Western forms of meditation xv–xvi, 5.
  See also Focused Attention Meditation
  (FAM); Open Monitoring Meditation
  (OMM)
*What Now? Meditation for Your Twenties and
  Beyond* (Shy) 81, 83
whole person 27
Wilber, Ken 115

*Working Memory, Fluid Intelligence, and
  Impulsiveness in Heavy Media
  Multitaskers* 24
writing, mindful 87

Yogananda (Swami Yogananda Giri) 6

Zen Buddhism 5, 81

Made in the USA
Coppell, TX
26 September 2023